Review copy,
wall street Journal
Sept. 1985

# The Nature and Logic
of Capitalism

*Books by Robert L. Heilbroner*

Marxism: For and Against

Beyond Boom and Crash

Business Civilization in Decline

An Inquiry into the Human Prospect

Between Capitalism and Socialism

The Economic Problem

The Limits of American Capitalism

A Primer on Government Spending
*(with Peter L. Bernstein)*

The Great Ascent

The Making of Economic Society

The Future as History

The Quest for Wealth

The Worldly Philosophers

*Robert L. Heilbroner*

# The Nature and Logic
# of Capitalism

W · W · NORTON & COMPANY

NEW YORK · LONDON

FIRST EDITION

The text of this book is composed in Times Roman, with display type set in Janson. Composition and manufacturing by The Haddon Craftsmen, Inc. Book design by Marjorie J. Flock.

Library of Congress Cataloging in Publication Data
Heilbroner, Robert L.
   The nature and logic of capitalism.

   Includes index.
   1. Capitalism.   I. Title.
HB501.H398   1985      330.12′2      85-5656

ISBN 0-393-02227-7

W. W. Norton & Company, Inc., 500 Fifth Avenue, New York, N.Y. 10110
W. W. Norton & Company Ltd., 38 Great Russell Street, London WC1B 3NU

1 2 3 4 5 6 7 8 9 0

# Contents

*Preface*                                                          9

### 1
On the Nature and Logic of Social Systems          13

### 2
The Drive to Amass Capital                                  33

### 3
The Regime of Capital                                         53

### 4
The Role of the State                                          78

### 5
The Ideology of Capital                                      107

### 6
The Logic of Capitalist Development                    141

### 7
The Limits of Social Analysis                             180

*Bibliography*                                                   209

*Index*                                                             215

Contents

# Preface

TWO MATTERS of some importance must be taken up before we can proceed to the substance of this inquiry into the nature and logic of the capitalist system. The first concerns the relation of the argument to that of Marx and the immense body of work that follows in his tradition. I dislike raising the question, but I do so for two reasons: first, because the answer will affect the response of many readers, positively or negatively, by virtue of the bright nimbus or the dark cloud that Marxism conjures up; and second, because the answer affects the level of exposition of the text.

Is this a Marxist view of capitalism? I am myself at a loss to give a clearcut answer to the question in view of the sprawling and disorganized state of what passes as a "Marxist" approach to social inquiry in general, or capitalism in particular. Much therefore depends on one's knowledge of that vast and ill-defined effort. For readers who will encounter for the first time the overall vision of capitalism that emerges in these pages, Marx's thought will no doubt appear as the single most pervasive and important influence. For others, more familiar with that thought and its elaboration within contemporary social science and history, what is apt to be noticeable are the distances and differences that separate my vision from that of much Marxian scholarship today and from Marx himself.[1]

The issue of the degree of Marxian purity or the absence of Marxian taint is deplorable in any case. I raise the question because the assumptions and lexicon of Marx's work are still unfamiliar to much of the educated American public, as well as to considerable numbers of social scientists. I have therefore had to spell out a number of points that will be elementary for those at home in the world of Marxian scholarship but that are nonetheless elemental and essential for my argument. The converse of this is that the Marxian approach to a number of central matters is anything but settled, so that utilizing its concepts has on more than one occasion involved my taking sides in contested issues. To elaborate on these disputes, or to justify my own position with regard to them, would take me far afield of my purpose. I have decided to pursue my course as if it traversed neutral ground, but I must inform the neophyte and admit to the scholar that I know I am sometimes riding roughshod over uncertainly held terrain.

A second general issue concerns the level of scholarly detail and documentation appropriate for the book. I cover a wide range of material: classical, Marxian, and contemporary economics; anthropological investigations into early civilization; psychoanalytically based speculations with regard to "human nature"; various aspects of

---

1. In my *Marxism: For and Against* (New York: W. W. Norton, 1980) I discuss these distances and differences, as well as the underlying filiations.

political and sociological theory; and of course a good deal of general and sometimes quite specific history. How much of this requires textual identification? I have come down on the side of spareness, citing specific quotations or important references but avoiding as much as possible long, discursive notes or a parade of well-known sources. I have, however, tried to identify contemporary works that have influenced me strongly, not only to pay my due respects but to forestall any appearance of posing as the author of ideas of which I am only an interpreter, or perhaps synthesizer.*

It is as difficult for me to know how much of the book is new as to know how much is "my own." Previous books of mine develop some parts of the argument that follows; other parts, and the overall architecture, are novel, or at least have never been put by me in quite this way before. The work as a whole moves at a stratospheric level of abstraction, very far removed from the rich microhistory that is the current vogue. How else could one hope to cover so vast a terrain? I have nonetheless tried to give the argument as much specificity as possible, without which it would not have the bite I intend for it. The book is, of course, written mainly in the context of the country in which I live, but the whole point of the study is to emphasize the second word in the phrase *American capitalism.* I have no expectations that this journey between heaven and earth will satisfy the dialectical angels looking down or the empirical earthlings looking up, and no delusions that the book will dispose of matters that have defied

---

*A short bibliography at the end will indicate my main sources and references.

resolution to this date and are likely to continue to defy it for a long time to come. With all these acknowledgments and anticipated defeats, this is my effort to put paid to questions that demand some kind of settlement, even if necessarily on provisional account.

Finally, as part of the matter of settling accounts, I must give proper thanks to a few people who have provided assistance at various stages of this project, some with expert guidance, all with their moral support. I shall begin by paying homage to Adolph Lowe, in his tenth decade still my intellectual example, grand critic, and invaluable Beckmesser. Anwar Shaikh, my colleague at the New School for Social Research, has given me searching criticisms and indispensable encouragement, for which I am deeply grateful. I am indebted for readings of earlier drafts and for learned assistance to Peter L. Bernstein, Ronald Blackwell, Joseph F. X. Kaufman, Sir Henry Lintott, and Henri Zukier, and to Laurence Malone for helpful suggestions. I am also thankful for a Guggenheim Fellowship that greatly facilitated the completion of the work. And as so often before, Lillian Salzman gave her loving care to readying the manuscript.

I reserve the last words for my wife, whose belief, skepticism, criticism, praise, impatience, endurance, and great solicitude were necessary conditions for seeing the work through.

# 1

# On the Nature and Logic of Social Systems

I HAVE CHOSEN a formal, even formidable, title for my book, and my first task is therefore to clarify what *The Nature and Logic of Capitalism* is about. Perhaps I can best do so by relating it to my previous work. For a long time I have conceived of my investigations into economics as the exploration of scenarios of development of capitalist economies. Scenario is a somewhat melodramatic, but I think apt, term, for it implies that the developmental sequences of capitalism depict narratives as well as impersonal processes—historical dramas that emerge most strikingly from the pages of *The Wealth of Nations* and *Capital* but that are discoverable to some degree in the works of most of the great economists.

Thirty years ago I presented these scenarios as the projects of the "worldly philosophers," and in later books I have used my own imagination to suggest likely trajectories of the system. Gradually, however, my focus of interest in economics has shifted. The evolution of capitalism continues to attract my attention, but I now see the object of my inquiries as directed at a larger question—not:

*What will become of capitalism?* but *What is capitalism?*
That is the profound and perplexing problem to which this
book is addressed.

Scenarios of economic change are problem-ridden for
many reasons, of which the most obvious, although perhaps not the most fundamental, is simply the number of
variables that enter into their determination. But the question of what capitalism "is" presents challenges of another
kind. Now the difficulty is not so much to cope with
masses of material as to decide on a few quintessential
elements. This is a much more recalcitrant question. The
variables that affect the capitalist process overwhelm us in
their complexity, but it is at least imaginable that they
might be coherently ordered. No such conceptual clarity
is available when it comes to determining the irreducible
elements of the system. No formal procedures, even at the
most abstract level, tell us how to specify the essence of
a thing.

Therefore we are left with a task for which no sure
guides and many alternatives exist. Is the irreducible core
of capitalism a distinctive arrangement of its social arrangements of production, a view that reflects Marx's famous taxonomy of history into "modes of production"?
Or does its essence lie in the realm of ideas rather than
material considerations, as Weber or Schumpeter would
maintain with their emphasis on the equally famous rational bourgeois mindset? Do we mean by capitalism a
single long evolutionary Western epoch that begins with
the rise of mercantile power in the seventeenth century
and continues to this day; or does capitalism have its own
discontinuities, completing a mercantile phase without

any inherent impetus into the next, then appearing in new guise as industrial capitalism, and now in our times assuming still new forms as "postindustrial" society, perhaps even as what we call democratic socialism?

There is no generally accepted method of deciding such questions. Thus, in writing about the nature and logic of capitalism, perhaps surprisingly the most problematical word is the last. In his immense panorama of economic life that leads from the late Middle Ages through the industrial revolution into modern times, the doyen of French economic historians, Fernand Braudel, mentions capitalism only in passing in his first volume, traces the etymology of *capital* and *capitalist* but not *capitalism* in his second volume, and manages to avoid an explicit definition of the term in his third, where capitalism appears as a congeries of trading and commercial activities, but is curiously absent in any sense of a clearly defined system or social order.[1]

It is easy to sympathize with Braudel's position. Twenty years ago I was myself so eager to avoid the difficulties of the term *capitalism* that I proposed relegating it to a kind of limbo and concentrating instead on the sharp particulars of the business system. Could we not, I asked, devote our attention to the immediate world of industrial enterprises, of market relationships, of commercial values and vocabularies—the specific attributes that allow individu-

---

1. Fernand Braudel, *Civilization and Capitalism,* 3 vols. (New York: Harper & Row, 1982, 1984). See reviews by Keith Thomas, *New York Review of Books,* November 22, 1984 and Lawrence Stone, *The New Republic,* October 1, 1984.

als from Sweden and Japan to "do business" with one another despite the differences in their social milieus—and thereby bypass the pitfalls of an abstract analysis by dealing with the concrete realities of business life?[2]

In more recent years, I have come to the conclusion that we cannot take this course. I no longer think it is possible to skirt the troublesome issue of defining capitalism by resort to more concrete, less contentious terms such as the business world or modern industrial society. Let me make the point by reexamining business life as I now see it. Without question, the business world represents the outward-facing reality of capitalism and is an inextricable part of whatever capitalism is. It is the presence of business firms and business practices, whether in the guise and habits of Dickensian London or modern-day New York, that constitutes the capitalism of daily life, the system in which men and women participate and by which they are directly affected. Yet there is another aspect to this familiar world, equally essential to its existence but not itself tangible or concrete. This is a kind of netherworld in whose grip the activities of business are caught. That netherworld may be called the Invisible Hand, or the laws of motion of the system, or the market mechanism; and its influence on the business world may be seen as propelling it in the direction of growth, involving it in internal contradictions, or guiding it toward a position of overall balance and stability. In every case, however, the business world itself is seen as a mere vehicle by which larger and

---

2. R. Heilbroner, *The Limits of American Capitalism* (New York: Harper & Row, 1966), pp. 4, 5.

more encompassing principles of order and movement are carried out.

It is, of course, precisely such an image of a world of everyday affairs, caught in the grip of forces that impel it willy-nilly toward some destination not of its own making, that constitutes the central fascination of capitalism for the great economists. For Adam Smith the force is that of  the Deity working its will to direct human action into socially beneficial paths that men could not discover for themselves with their limited capacity for reason and foresight. To Marx the directing agency is an internal dialectic that asserts its sway through a "fetishism" that blinds men to their real social situation, causing them to see only iron exchanging against linen in the marketplace, not relationships of labor and capital governing market transactions from behind the scene. For modern economics the ordering impulse originates in the efforts of individuals to acquire material wealth against the counterpressures of others within the confines of the social and physical world—a drama of drive and constraint that impels the larger society toward a destination depicted as a "general equilibrium" of wants and capabilities.

In every case, however, the activities of business—in so many ways the very epitome of independently conceived and purposefully motivated action—are perceived as obeying imperatives that originate below the surface of daily economic life. The structuring effect that this netherworld casts over the course of business activity is never precisely revealed in the pattern of economic events, any more than the design produced by a magnet in the arrangement of iron filings exactly reveals the arcs and loops of its field of force. Yet in the one case as in the other, the persisting presence of an order-bestowing influence is felt. A tap of history's finger disrupts the clear manifestation of the Invisible Hand, the laws of motion, the tendency to general equilibrium, or whatever, but as business activities repeat themselves day after day, the background pattern again becomes evident, just as the force field of magnetism reveals itself most clearly when filings are poured afresh onto one sheet of paper after the other.

This image serves as well as any to convey why I have come to see the scenarios of the great economists as depicting more than sequences of economic states or the dynamics of economic change. Consciously or otherwise, their scenarios are also representations of another level of reality—a level of "nether" pressures and processes expressed through a variety of visible drives and institutions. From this point of view, their scenarios are not only projections as to what capitalism may become but conceptions of what capitalism is—that is, descriptions of a social order that manifests its historic trajectory because it is in the thrall of specific forces or determinative agencies. As we shall shortly see, this general description can be applied to all "social formations," the somewhat unfamiliar but useful term by which Marx distinguishes the major structural epochs of history. It is here that I take my own departure into the investigation of these formations by describing the trajectory of these systems as their logic, and the forces or determinative agencies as their nature, so that I shall speak of capitalism as that social order in which a certain kind of nature gives rise to an historically unique logic.

## II

As a first approximation, then, let us take the nature of capitalism as referring to its behavior-shaping institutions and relationships, and the logic of capitalism as the pattern of configurational change generated and guided by this inner core. Both nature and logic are needed to conceptualize the historic totality of any system. Just as we have seen that a description directed only at the business aspects of the capitalist world fails to capture its ordered properties, so a description aimed solely at the invisible force fields within the system would fail to convey its sense of motion, its guided historical path.

I hope these words convey a general sense of what a logic and nature of capitalism imply, but I am certain they raise as many questions as they answer. I propose therefore that we proceed at once to a deeper examination of our mode of analysis by examining the idea of the nature and logic of social formations in general, not just those of capitalism. We shall leave aside a definition of these formations, for the gradual clarification of our understanding will yield as one of its results a better criterion for periodizing history into large-scale categories of one kind or another. For the moment I ask only that we accept the conventional distinctions among societies that can be described as primitive, imperial, feudal, and capitalist, with full awareness of the difficulties of drawing precise boundaries around them and of the variations of institutions within them.

With our critical impulses temporarily held in check, let us plunge into the argument by pursuing further the idea of the "nature" of a social formation. The term refers to the ensemble of elements that influence the behavior of its members, especially those kinds of behavior that drive the system along a particular historical path. Here are, to begin, the givens of geography, climate, and natural setting that exert their silent but continuous pressures on the lives lived within their ambit, brilliantly illustrated, for instance, in the opening chapters of Braudel's work on the Mediterranean world.[3] These geographic and climatic givens are often decisive in determining the variants of a social formation that are compatible with the environment, or in encouraging or blocking the social organizations characteristic of certain formations. As with all animals, humans must adapt to their environment, although the possibility exists, as the technical powers of society increase, for humans to adapt their environment to themselves. At any rate, these geographic givens play only a minor role in constituting the behavioral patterns that give to capitalism its nature, although it is obvious that geography and resources play a very important part in delimiting the field of opportunities against which the capitalist logic unfolds.

Far more important as an active force in the behavior-shaping core of social systems are the drives and capacities of the human animal as a species being. What interests us here are not the physical endowments of the newborn child—its sensory equipment, its motor and other instincts, its language propensities, etc.—but the psychic endowments that play critical roles in the transformation

---

3. Fernand Braudel, *The Mediterranean,* Vol I (New York: Harper & Row, 1972), Chs. 1–4.

of the neonate into the socialized adult. Among these endowments are the universal necessity for the bestowal and receipt of libidinal energy or affect; the capacity for conscious and unconscious fantasy; narcissistic and aggressive impulses; Oedipal conflicts and still other primordial and inexpungeable attributes of the psyche. This array of powerful thrustings and receptivities is as integral to humankind as its genetic equipment, and of much greater importance in shaping its behavior individually and collectively.

The linkage between the energies of the individual psyche and the mass behavior of people is much less well understood than that between the unconscious and the individual. Nevertheless, the central theme of Freud's work—the persistence into adulthood of infantile dependency traits and the idealization of parental surrogates—provides essential insights into phenomena of history and society that are otherwise inexplicable. There are, for instance, the universal creation of distinctions of social prestige; the surrender of self into ceremonies and mass activities and beliefs; the indifference to or enjoyment of cruelties inflicted on humans who are classified as "others" rather than "brothers"; and similar manifestations and susceptibilities of human behavior en masse.* The

---

*Freud's most direct discussion of the relation between individual psychoanalytic dynamics and collective social action remains his *Group Psychology and the Analysis of the Ego*. There are also well-known remarks in *The Future of an Illusion, Civilization and its Discontents, Thoughts on War,* and elsewhere, but nothing like a systematic discussion of the problem exists in his work. I am indebted to Dr. David Beres and to Professors Henri Zukier and Peter Gay for various psychoanalytic references. Finally, I must call attention to a pioneering study by Harold Lasswell, "The Triple Appeal Principle: A Contribution of Psychoanalysis to Political and Social Science," *American Journal of Sociology,* January 1932.

vulnerability of human motive and action to the demands of the unconscious can be ignored only by reducing all social behavior to "rational action," or by relegating it to the inexplicable. To my mind this general vulnerability provides the scientific basis for what is often called "human nature," and it is with this meaning that I shall invoke these words in discussing the roots of social behavior in capitalism as well as in other social systems.

In our next chapter we shall have occasion to look more carefully into certain aspects of human nature. At this juncture we must still trace out further aspects of the behavior-shaping social core. Now we move from the level of physical and psychic endowments toward the surface of society, where we find its institutions and organizations and belief systems, the vessels of its culture. These are the social forms into which primal energies must be poured— forms that themselves have been created in part to respond to these very energies but that now act as channels for their social direction.

It would be impossible to make a systematic inventory of these institutions. Any such attempt, however, would have to give prominence to two categories. One of these consists of the inherited technical capability of the community, embedded in its implements of production and its stores of knowledge—the material aspect of Marx's "forces of production." This sociotechnical apparatus is itself open to change, especially under the dynamics of capitalism, but at any moment it establishes powerful enablements and limitations that guide the behavior of individuals, above all in what we call "economic life." Technology therefore plays a role not unlike that of the natural setting itself, save that the material artifacts of the man-made environment are much more malleable than those of climate or geography. Thus, in considering the elements that shape behavior, in play and war as well as in work, the tool and the machine and the general level of material capability are as powerful as the lay of the land and its riches—indeed more powerful in that technology can re-shape the land and create riches where there was only desert.

Of at least equal importance with the institutions that shape the economic activities of the system are those that mold behavior and belief at the diffuse, unspecialized level we call social life. Here, typical behavioral ways are influenced by the pressures of indoctrination and education —experiences that make it possible for individuals to enter their social formations with a sense of familiarity and acceptance. These pressures begin with the family that introduces the infant to the norms of private and public existence; continue with the reinforcement of, and some-times with the challenge to, those norms by the child's peers and teachers; and are capped by the enticements, rewards and punishments administered by larger social organizations, from churches to corporations to the state itself. The latter includes, of course, the socio-legal frame-work that casts its powerful compulsions over so much of social activity, establishing with the force of law what we must do and what we may not do.

This socializing and normalizing process is by no means a completely integrated or frictionless one. As they move through history, all societies must make their peace with nature and with themselves, the latter constituting the theme of domination and oppression that will play a very large role in our analysis. Here we need only note that the institutions in which are molded typical patterns of rule, obedience, and beliefs are themselves molded by an inner dynamic that may take the form of class against class, against tribe, even civilization against civilization, or at times contests that focus on color, religion, sex.

For these reasons, at close range the socialization process is often a tense and sometimes turbulent one. But at a sufficient historic distance, the spectrum of socializing institutions clearly succeeds in creating typical behavioral patterns. Primitive societies produce hunters and gatherers with their requisite attitudes as well as skills; imperial and feudal societies produce peasants and lords with their respective mentalities and accepted roles; and capitalist societies create workers and capitalists who also bring to their activities deeply ingrained conceptions of their social functions. Were there not a high degree of dependability to this indoctrination process, the extraordinary stability of social formations would not be the rule, and humanity would long ago have perished or found its way to a heaven on earth. The viscosity that is so prominent a feature of social history must therefore be traced to the stabilizing influence of the behavior-shaping cores of its social formations.

### III

Let me turn now to an initial consideration of the idea of the "logic" of a social formation, the consequence of the forces and institutions that give it its nature. Need I interject that this is not an Aristotelian logic of mathematical certitude? I use the word in a causal sense—a logic of situations, of human outcomes. Thus the logic of a social formation refers to the movements of and changes in the "life processes" and institutional configurations of a society. What is "logical" about these movements is that they express the outcome of the system's nature, as a released spring expresses the energy stored up within it. Wherever there is social movement there is a matrix of shaping influences whence this movement issues. Societies steering through uncharted waters depend as much on the cooperation of a willing—or cowed—crew as on the force of leadership, so that even the most daring historical journeys have their logics in the forces and institutions without which these adventures would not be possible.

A system's logic therefore expresses the potential energy created by its nature. This potential energy is discharged in innumerable processes and can be considered at many levels of complexity—in capitalism, for instance, in terms of the operation of a single market or of a market "mechanism." For the time being, however, we will consider only the "grand logic" of social formations—the logic manifested in the rise and fall of their class structures or in the most far-reaching changes of their institutions. These major movements are most easily discerned in the case of capitalism, where the logic of the system takes such systemic forms as changing profiles of material output, patterns of employment, or class distributions of income. With earlier societies in which the economic aspect of life played a much less independent role, there is no such strikingly measureable aspect of the system's logic, for their economies did not present the ordered sequences of change that are of such importance under capitalism.

But even under capitalism, it is clear that economic variables in themselves comprise only a portion of the historic drama played out by the system. The evolving sociopolitical configuration of capitalism, as it moves from the pre-industrial landscape of Adam Smith to that of the contemporary "post-industrial" state, certainly reflects the impact of economic forces, but equally certainly it involves the effect of political and ideological developments, where the role of economic elements can often only be located in the background. And certainly in tracing the histories of imperial kingdoms or feudal principalities or primitive communities, the aspects of the narrative that command our attention and that most stand in need of explanation have very little if anything to do with self-directing economic sequences.

The logic of social formations is not therefore merely a playing-out of economic movements that arise from their behavior-shaping nature. Rather, the grand logic of societies embraces all large-scale and long-lasting institutional or cultural changes that arise from whatever source. These changes are not always easy to identify or explain—history is full of ill-understood or ill-explained logics, such as the fall of the Roman Empire, the decline of Mayan civilization, or for that matter the rise of capitalism. The idea of a logic of social formations is not, then, an attempt to reduce history's complexities to simple causal linkages, above all economic linkages. Rather, the idea suggests that patterned changes in history cannot be explained or understood without reference to the nature of the social formation that gives rise to specific behavioral and attitudinal characteristics. Even in so modest a form, such a hypothesis is bound to raise objections and caveats. As with the concept of the nature of a social formation, I ask that we reserve our skepticism until the idea can be examined in more concrete form in the chapters to follow, including at the very end some reflections on the critical words *explain* and *understand.*

For the moment, however, let us illustrate the notion of a logic with a few very general examples. We can commence with primitive society, generalizing from the tattered remnants of what was once the main, perhaps the only, form of human community. These primitive societies have been described as having no history. By this we mean that they achieve immortality without leaving behind a narrative "written" in terms of a systematic evolution in their modes of subsistence, their structures of authority, their belief systems, or even their adventures. To put the matter more cautiously, if there are such changes or adventures, they do not reveal an immanent directing impulse, so that these societies appear to sleepwalk through time.

Yet such societies also display a nature and logic, although of a completely different kind from that with which we have heretofore been concerned. In their case it is the very changelessness of the structure of primitive life that is the salient aspect of its logic; and as is always the case, it is the elements that support and generate this requisite inert behavior that comprise its nature. Without in any way intending to be exhaustive, these inertial elements include a material relation to the environment that renders continuous technical experimentation dangerous or unnecessary; a structure of authority that minimizes tensions through the avoidance of exploitative relationships; a community that creates strong social obligations through kinship and reciprocity ties; and perhaps belief systems that discourage skepticism or other causes of intellectual ferment.[4]

In similar fashion we can apply the concept of a nature and logic to the array of empires, kingdoms, and despotisms to which Samir Amin has given the illumining title "tributary systems."[5] These societies typically display logics that are vastly more dynamic and complex than those of primitive communities, with a higher degree of adventure in their narratives and often with substantial material or political structural change. These logics in turn are the historical consequence of social systems in which institutions typically magnify the persona of a single person into a godlike ruler, the society then becoming a direct extension of the person of the shah, emperor, or king. This simple statement already gives some explanatory insight into what otherwise appears only as a meaningless array of personal achievements and failures, triumphs and disasters. The logic of tributary systems must be seen as the translation into "history" of the biographies of their central personages, the translation reflecting the vast numbers of lives affected by the will and character of the ruler.

In turn, of course, this suggests the need to look for forces and institutions that support such a despotic form

---

4. See Stanley Diamond, *In Search of the Primitive* (New Brunswick, N.J.: Transactions Books, 1974), Ch. 4.

5. Samir Amin, *Class and Nation* (New York: Monthly Review Press, 1980), Ch. 3.

of society. This brings us to consider the role played by human nature in establishing and perpetuating oppressive social relationships, a matter about which we will have more to say in our next chapter. Suffice it here merely to comment that the trappings of rule as well as the exercise of force revive infantile feelings of dependency, making possible the personality cult that is a central aspect of the nature of these societies, and the source of their biographical logics.

As one evidence of the fact that biographical histories have a logic—an explicable, understandable sequence in their unfoldings—consider their obsession with dynastic alliances. To someone to whom the nature of these societies remains unclear, the ceaseless quest for appropriate marriages and family successions seems only a tale of personal ambition. But from within a society where personal rulership is the central order-bestowing force, the necessity of securing a legitimate heir becomes as pressing and self-evident as that of securing a legitimate succession to the "person" of a corporation in the modern business world. The nature of tributary societies derives in large part from institutions that buttress and legitimate that imperial idea. The restless and imperative search for dynastic alliances thereby expresses more than the idiosyncratic marital or political ambitions of their rulers. It is a scenario fully as explicable in terms of behavioral regularities, and as understandable in terms of empathetic considerations, as the scenarios of societies driven by the "imperatives" of wealth.[6]

---

6. See Perry Anderson, *Lineages of the Absolutist State* (London: New Left Books, 1974), p. 39.

## IV

This brings us to capitalism, but I will postpone for the coming chapters a consideration of what nature and logic reveal about that familiar and yet strange social formation. Rather, let me conclude this introductory chapter with a last remark about the property of historic logics in general. The passage of societies through time does not take place in a vacuum, like the free fall of an object in space. Rather, as we have noted, social logics often generate frictions that alter the course of their trajectories in flight. The frictions arise because the behavioral-shaping cores of social formations—at least those beyond primitive society—are typically made up of institutions that reproduce the antagonistic interests or beliefs of different groups or social classes. As a consequence, a social formation is rarely able to move changelessly through history, reproducing without end its initial configuration of material, political, or cultural institutions and relationships but is likely to veer from this path as the clash and struggle among contending interests reshapes the underlying institutions themselves.

At the most obvious level, the existing behavioral forces may directly alter the environment by the conquest of foreign territories or by the redesign of the apparatus of production in ways that make impossible the continued pursuit of older routines and lifeways. At a more repressed level, the inability of a social formation to accommodate the wants of substantial portions of the population may result in the accumulation of resentments that lead ultimately to social concessions, perhaps to violent change. It need hardly be said that capitalism, with the extraordinary dynamism manifested in all spheres of its life, is par excellence the social formation in which the logic of the system affects its nature; but to some degree this is the case with all social systems that generate large-scale changes of any kind. That is why I must emphasize again that neither its nature nor its logic alone will give us an adequate grasp of what a society "is," which must include what it was, as well as what it might become.

Finally, let us return to a question posed in our initial section. Is there a need for the word *capitalism?* The perspective of nature and logic clarifies the question. The descriptive words by which we demarcate types of social formations, such as primitive or tributary societies, are useful only insofar as they bring to the forefront aspects of these formations that establish important resemblances within each ideal type, as well as distinctions among them. We speak of primitive society, fully aware of the differences between Eskimo, Trobriander, and Bushman, because there are common aspects of those societies that override these differences, knitting them into a common family of primitive communities. The idea of a nature and logic proposes that we establish these resemblances or differences in two interlinked aspects: according to the different trajectories—the logics—of the great social formations, and in the different inner natures from which these logics emerge.

It is beyond argument that the nature and logic of those societies we commonly call capitalist are profoundly at variance with those of primitive or imperial or feudal societies. The nature of capitalism, evidenced not only in its business institutions but in the general behavioral dispositions and beliefs that make its institutions "work," cannot be found in earlier forms of social organization; and the logic of capitalism, with its dramatic economic scenarios, similarly has no earlier parallel. A social formation that gives rise to such a distinctive life history assuredly deserves an identifying label that will call to attention the source of its unique momentum and character.

# 2

# The Drive to Amass Capital

WE MUST BEGIN by investigating the single most important element in capitalism—an element visible in the logic enacted by the world of business but originating deep within the system as an essential and indeed primary aspect of its behavioral orientation. This is the driving need to extract wealth from the productive activities of society *in the form of capital.*

The extraction of wealth, as a flow of "surplus" production systematically channeled from the broad working body of society into the hands of a restricted group or class, is by no means peculiar to capitalism. Surplus itself, in all societies, refers to the difference between the volume of production needed to maintain the work force and the volume of production the work force produces. It is not always easy to measure this difference with exactitude, or to compare one surplus with another when the two are embodied in different kinds of goods. But the general notion of a margin over and above that required for the maintenance—the "reproduction"—of society is a basic concept of classical political economy that offers no stumbling block.[1]

We discover surplus in all societies that have made the leap from primitive communities into civilizations, a leap that is universally associated with the rise of some form of centralized state. Indeed, a principal aspect of, and perhaps reason for, the formation of these states has been precisely the facilitation of the extraction of surplus. From the greatly enhanced organizational capacities of the state arose the colossal citadels and monumental works of Egypt and Persia, the Incan and Mayan empires, the dynastic kingdoms of India and China.

There is, however, a decisive difference between the character of the surplus products of these tributary societies and that of capitalism. In precapitalist societies surpluses assume the aspect of "wealth"—of desired objects—because they embody specific attributes that inhere in their physical characteristics. Wealth appears in such forms as goods or services devoted to luxury consumption, to the maintenance and deployment of armed force, to religious edifices, or simply to display. Wealth thereby takes on the properties of "use values," to use the term that Marx adopts from Adam Smith and Aristotle, including not least the use value of expressing the might and grandeur of rulership itself.

Conspicuously absent from these means of utilizing wealth is its application for a purpose central to, and indeed constitutive of, capitalism. *This is the use of wealth*

---

1. See, for example, Adam Smith, *The Wealth of Nations* (Oxford: Clarendon Press, 1976), p. 497. Smith calls the surplus the "balance of the annual produce and consumption."

*in various concrete forms, not as an end in itself, but as a*
*means for gathering more wealth.* The closest analogue to
this, in ancient kingdoms, is the employment of military
or religious or regal institutions and equipages, not merely
as symbols of power and prestige desired for their own
sakes but as instruments for military, religious, or dynastic
expansion. We shall shortly see that there are more than
superficial resemblances between this expansive use of surplus and that of capitalism, the common tie being the
utilization of surplus to augment the power of a dominant
class. Nevertheless, in ancient civilizations wealth itself is
represented mainly by physical embodiments that are its
sufficient reason for being, its final purpose.

In contrast, in capitalism wealth inhabits material things
only transiently. Thus Braudel is not correct when he
writes: "capital or capital goods, *which come to the same*
*thing* [my italics], can be divided into two categories: fixed
capital which has a long or fairly long *physical* life . . .;
and variable, working, or circulating capital . . . which is
absorbed and swallowed up in the production process:
seed-corn, raw materials, semi-finished products, the
money for all the various settlements of accounts."[2] This
has the ring of easy familiarity, but it leads us away from
rather than toward an understanding of what capital is. If
capital were only goods used in production or money
needed to buy materials and labor, then capital would be
as old as civilization, and there would be no purpose in
singling it out as an identifying element of one kind of
society, worthy of becoming, in fact, its historic badge. It

---

2. Fernand Braudel, *The Mediterranean*, Volume II, 1973, p. 242.

is precisely the failure to recognize this distinctive aspect of capital that leads Braudel to the curiously indifferent attitude to capitalism that I have noted earlier. It is a failure shared by conventional economics as well, which treats capital as a material category of things, or as money, and which accords to it no special properties that would explain why the social formation in which we live is described as the "ism" of capital.

What is capital, then, if it is not just production goods or money? The initial answer, familiar to students of Marx but usually strange to others, is that capital is either of these things when it is used to set into motion a process of continuous transformation of capital-as-money into capital-as-commodities, followed by a retransformation of capital-as-commodities into capital-as-more-money. This is the famous M-C-M' formula by which Marx schematized the repetitive, expansive metamorphosis through which "capital" manifests itself.

This repetitive, expansive process is, to be sure, directed at bringing goods and services into being through the organization of trade and production. But the physical attributes of those commodities, even when they take the form of luxurious objects, are not prized as evidences of a successful completion of the search for wealth, as long as they are in the capitalist's possession. On the contrary, their physical existence is an obstacle that must be overcome by converting the commodities back into money. Even then, when they are sold, the cash in turn is not regarded as the end product of the search but only as a stage in its never-ending cycle.

*Capital is therefore not a material thing but a process*

*that uses material things as moments in its continuously dynamic existence.* It is, moreover, a social process, not a physical one. Capital can, and indeed must, assume physical form, but its meaning can only be grasped if we perceive these material objects as embodying and symbolizing an expanding totality. A human being cannot exist without flesh and blood, but the essence of humanness is that flesh and blood are in the service of an organizing purpose, a life force. So it is with capital. Without the organizing purpose of expansion, capital dissolves into material building blocks that are necessary but not sufficient to define its life purpose.

The relation of money and capital is particularly interesting in that money is the closest that wealth comes under capitalism to finding an analogue to the use values in which it appears in older societies. It is the way in which we usually measure the extent of capital, especially for an individual capitalist or firm. Yet, as we have just seen, money in itself is not capital: it is money-in-use that is capital. Money has served this capital-like function even before capitalism appeared, for example when merchants in antiquity used it to hire casual hands to carry wares or to man a ship. In these cases, too, money served as capital —that is, as an intermediary in a process whose aim was the merchant's capacity to carry on an M-C-M' circuit in trade. The only reason we do not designate these ancient societies as capitalist is that the production or trade-guiding functions of these nuclei of capital were minuscule compared with tradition and command, the main renewing or directing forces within these systems. Capitalist processes in these societies were therefore relegated to the periphery of social activity, often directing luxury-oriented activities but never central or crucial ones.

The analysis of capital as an expansive process is an important step in escaping from the fetishism of capital as objects, such as machines, or as a sum of money. It leads us to see capital as a web of social activities that permit the continuous metamorphosis of M-C-M′ to take place. At the center of this process is a social relationship between the *owners* of money and goods, the momentary embodiments of capital, and the *users* of these embodiments, who need them to carry on the activity of production on which their own livelihoods depend. The legal crux of this relationship lies in the right of exclusion: a central, although often ignored, meaning of "property" is that its owners can legally refuse to allow their possessions to be used by others. The critical aspect of money or capital goods as private property does not lie in the right of owners to use them in any way they wish, for such a dangerous social right has never existed, but to withhold them from use if their owners see fit. It is this right that enables the capitalist to dominate the sphere of trade and production in which his authority extends, as other legal rights enable military officers or priests or political figures to dominate the spheres in which their authority extends.

The idea of capital as a social relationship leads directly to the core of that relationship: *domination.* Here we must immediately note a striking difference between the domination exercised by owners of capital and that belonging to "owners" of other aspects of social authority. It is that the domination of the army, the church, and of course the state derives its behavior-shaping powers directly from the use or threat of physical or spiritual punishment, up to and including death or its spiritual equivalent. That is, it is within the legal competence of these authorities to inflict pains directly on those who fail to obey their commands. The process of socialization may make it sufficient merely to display the symbols of power, not to wield its might, but the capacity to utilize force or to inflict suffering remains the essence of the capacity for domination.

The power wielded by capital differs in subtle but substantial ways. The owner of capital is not entitled to use direct force against those who refuse to enter into engagement with him as buyer or seller. The merchant or the industrial employer may, of course, have recourse to the power of the state to enforce contractual arrangements, and the state is usually—although not always or by legal necessity—willing to lend its punitive powers to break strikes, disband picketers, provide armed guards to protect the routes and outposts of trade or the establishments of production. Nonetheless, the coercive force itself belongs to the state, not to the capitalist; and when the capitalist employs strong-arm tactics it is a usurpation, not a proper use of power.

In a word, there is a qualitative difference between the power of an institution to wield the knout, to brand, mutilate, deport, chain, imprison, or execute those who defy its will, and the power of an institution to withdraw its support, no matter how life-giving that support may be. Even if we imagined that all capital was directed by a single capitalist, the sentence of starvation that could be passed by his refusal to sell his commodities or to buy labor power differs from the sentence of the king who casts his opponents into a dungeon to starve, because the capitalist has no legal right to forbid his victims from moving elsewhere, or from appealing to the state or other authorities against himself.

Thus the domination of the merchant, for instance, resides in his legal right not to sell to those who will not meet his price—a right that can involve great social deprivation, as in the case of a famine, but that is nonetheless entirely free of direct personal coercion: the merchant cannot require a potential buyer to become an actual one. Similarly, the domination of an industrial capitalist is immediately limited to his right not to offer employment to those who will not accept his terms—again, a right that can carry the most severe consequences but whose exercise is devoid of the punitive confrontation of officer and soldier, priest and communicant, ruler and subject. However harsh the domination of capital may be, it therefore always operates at a remove, and with a degree of voluntary submission implicit in the potential refusal of the other party to accept the capitalist's terms, an option generally absent from precapitalist modes of domination. Conventional economists recoil at the unaccustomed idea of capital as a relationship of domination, but Marxian economists too often forget that the domination represented by capital emancipates society from harsher previous modes of domination.

What is of importance for our present focus is that capital can exert its organizing and disciplining influence only when social conditions make the withholding of capital an act of critical social consequence. This obviously entails in the first instance the rise of a capital-oriented class—originally always the merchant class—from a subordinate position within society to a position of leverage. This is the result of the merchants' capture of increasingly strategic social functions, from the financing of rulers to the provisioning of cities. No less important, the domination of capital hinges on the appearance of a class of workers who are dependent for their livelihood on access to the tools and land that can be legally denied to them by their owners. Adam Smith saw this dependency: "Many workmen could not subsist a week, few could subsist a month, and scarce any a year without employment," he writes. "In the long-run the workman may be as necessary to his master as his master is to him, but the necessity is not so immediate."[3]

What Smith did not see was the point stressed by Marx: the dependency also presupposed the dissolution of previous social relationships in which the peasant was entitled by law and custom to retain some portion of the crops he directly raised, and in which the urban worker owned his own means of production in the form of a cottage loom, a potter's wheel, and the like. That altered relationship was the end product of a protracted revolution, commencing in the fifteenth century or even earlier, continuing through the nineteenth, and in some parts of the world still in progress, in which the enclosure movement, the destruction of protected crafts and guilds, the creation of a proletariat from the cellars of society, and the whirlwind forces of new technologies disrupted the social relations of

---

3. Smith, *Wealth of Nations,* p. 84.

older socioeconomic regimes and prepared the way for the wholly different regime of capital.

However varied the agencies of this immense revolution, its effect was always the same: established rights of direct access to one's own product were replaced by new rights by which peasants and workers were legally excludable from access to their means of livelihood. Only by understanding that the seemingly concrete entity of capital is in fact the representation of this relationship of dependency between two different categories of social existence can the significance of capital be grasped, and with it the behavioral influence that it exerts as a central constitutive element in the nature of the system erected in its name.

## II

The relationship of domination has two poles. One of them—the social dependency of propertyless men and women without which capital could not exert its organizing influence—has been exhaustively studied by historians, particularly for the period during which feudal relations give way to capitalist ones.[4] Here I want to turn to the other, less examined pole—the restless and insatiable drive to accumulate capital.

What is the rationale of this endless process? Adam Smith found the answer in the social approval that riches drew to their possessor: "The rich man glories in his

---

4. The literature of proletarianization begins with Marx's famous chapters on "primitive accumulation" (*Capital,* I, Part 8 [New York: Vintage, 1977]) but has long since lost its exclusive Marxian character. See the classic account by Paul Mantoux, *The Industrial Revolution in the 18th Century* (London: Jonathan Cape, 1952).

riches, because he feels that they naturally draw upon him the attention of the world. . . . At the thought of this, his heart seems to swell and dilate itself within him, and he is fonder of his wealth, upon this account, than for all the other advantages it procures him."[5]

Smith's answer points in the direction of what seems to be a universal element in all societies, the desire for prestige and distinction. If we inquire more deeply into the etiology of prestige itself, we must probably look toward the universal need for affect, the consequence of the prolonged human nurturant experience, or to a sublimated form of the sexual drive for preeminence that is part of the genetic endowment of all living beings.

Prestige or distinction are gained in many ways—among them, strength, bravery, intelligence, wisdom, or the reputed possession of magical or other special powers. These are qualitative attributes of individuals and have little or nothing to do with the possession of goods or even of rights. It is a general fact, however, that the distinction of prestige is associated in many societies with a special category of "prestige goods," such as the cattle of the African herders, which confer distinction on their owners, regardless of whatever personal characteristics they may have.[6] It is this capacity of inanimate things to enhance the personae of their owners that is of interest to us in seeking the roots of the unbounded drive to amass wealth as capi-

---

5. Smith, *Theory of Moral Sentiments* (Oxford: Clarendon Press, 1976), pp. 50–51.

6. For prestige and prestige goods, see Morton Fried, *The Evolution of Political Society* (New York: Random House, 1976) and Marshall Sahlins, *Stone Age Economics* (Hawthorne, N.Y.: Aldine, 1972).

tal. It is uncertain whether all societies possess prestige goods, but there is no question that all humankind possesses the capacity, rooted in infantile narcissism, to project psychic energies and fantasies into objects that then become extensions or embellishments of the person him or herself. As William James noted long ago, "Between what a man calls me and he calls *mine,* the line is very difficult to draw." Marx, too, recognized this attribute when he wrote, "The extent of the power of money is the extent of my power. Money's properties are my properties and essential powers—the properties and powers of its possessor."[7]

The importance of prestige goods lies in their dramatizion of an essential precondition in human nature for the existence of "wealth." The desire to accumulate capital has other roots, as we shall see, but prestige and distinction are certainly prominent elements, much as Adam Smith described them. If we have gone beyond Smith or Marx in this regard, it is only insofar as we can link the need for preeminence to the unconcious levels of the personality, and to the degree that we recognize the universal human capacity to treat things as extensions of the person.

The drive for prestige, however, is only a necessary, not a sufficient condition of the drive for wealth. For wealth differs in a crucial respect from prestige objects, or from the possession of personal distinction. Prestige and distinction enlarge the authority and repute of their posses-

7. William James, *Principles of Psychology,* Vol. I (New York: Henry Holt, 1890), pp. 291–92; Marx, "The Power of Money in Bourgeois Society," in *Economic and Philosophic Manuscripts of 1844* (New York: International Publishers, 1964), p. 167.

sors but not necessarily their ability to force others to do their bidding. The power of community headmen, for example, is notoriously weak,[8] as is that of many prestigious figures in modern society, such as its moral or intellectual leaders. On occasion moral authority has huge power, but as a rule its capacity to control social action is small.

The attribute of wealth that distinguishes it from prestige goods is that its possession confers on its owners the ability to direct and mobilize the activities of society, although it does not necessarily also confer the repute or authority of distinction. Capital calls the tune, even though an individual capitalist may be an object of contempt. Wealth therefore implies rights of a kind that prestige objects do not have, in particular those we have previously discussed with respect to the domination of capital —namely, the right of denying to others access to the goods that constitute wealth. These goods may enjoy no symbolic importance, but they have material importance, so that control over access to them invests their owner with an attribute that goes beyond prestige and preeminence. This is power. The grain in the lord's granary is not an object of prestige, as is the splinter of the Cross in his chapel, but it is the means by which he is able to command the labor of his slaves, which the splinter of the Cross may not.

*Wealth is therefore a social category inseparable from power.* In simple egalitarian societies, where all have access to the resources needed for the maintenance of a

---

8. Fried, *Evolution of Political Society,* p. 68; Sahlins, *Stone Age Economics,* p. 98.

conventional way of life, wealth cannot exist, although prestige objects can. Per contra, wealth can only come into existence when the right of access of all members of society to an independent livelihood no longer prevails, so that control over this access becomes of life-giving importance. The corollary is that wealth cannot exist unless there also exists a condition of scarcity—not insufficiency of resources themselves, but insufficiency of means of access to resources. As Adam Smith put it, "Wherever there is great property, there is great inequality. For one very rich man, there must be at least five hundred poor, and the affluence of the rich supposes the indigence of the many."[9]

## III

Unlike the simpler category of prestige goods, wealth therefore rests on considerations of power, and the drive to accumulate wealth requires some exploration of the drive to accumulate power.

Power is not a well-understood aspect of human society. Essentially it refers to the ability to command or control the behavior of others; but this general definition passes lightly over the great range of relationships expressed in the power of the despot, the religious leader, or in the disembodied "power" of ideas. The power of capital, as we have seen, has the remarkable attribute of being devoid of direct punitive rights, which seems virtually a contradiction of the very meaning of power; but none would deny that capital has the power to enlist command and obedience on a vast scale.

9. Smith, *Wealth of Nations*, pp. 709–710.

Power is not only protean in its aspects but obscure in its psychic roots. The "pleasures" of power are usually assumed to exist but are not explained; and the interrelation between the exercise of will as power and the acceptance of that will as obedience is similarly left unexplored. Here, as with prestige, it seems necessary to find some anchorage in those psychosocial capacities of the species to which we give the name "human nature." It is tempting to suggest that at some elemental level this anchorage links the phenomenon of "domination" in human society with that found in many animal species. On second look, however, we see that the word refers to entirely different aspects of the two worlds.[10] Domination among animals is largely sexual in nature, probably associated with survival chances for the herd or troop or flock, and completely divorced from any division of tasks or general subservience to the "will" of a hegemonic individual. Domination in human society, on the other hand, is of minor evolutionary significance, and largely devoted to the division of the social product or to the fulfillment of the prestige-laden achievements of rulers for which the organized labor of large numbers is necessary. Domination in human society, in a word, entails a structured inequality of life conditions that has no parallel in the animal world.

The only reason that filiation with animal "domination" continues to attract attention is the need to explain why this inequality, which grossly disadvantages the majority, has appeared in every quarter of the globe, displacing the egalitarian social structures of communal

---

10. See the discussion in Sahlins, *The Use and Abuse of Biology* (Ann Arbor, Mich.: University of Michigan Press, 1976), Ch. 1.

bands that anthropologists assume to have been the original social formation. If the prevalance of domination in human societies cannot without gross anthropomorphism be ascribed to residual "animal" tendencies, we must account for this all-important historical state of affairs by resort to purely human characteristics. Here, of course, is where human nature enters, in the role of the generally acknowledged significance of prolonged infantile dependency, the uniquely and universally human experience out of which social behavior is formed.

In this experience the individual personage goes through successive rites of passage that gradually and painfully separate it from an original psychic fusion with its mother and immediate environment. Through these inescapable trials the potentialities of independent behavior are created, but so also are the encapsulizations of infantile emotional requirements and sadomasochistic drives that recede, but are never extinguished, within the adult person. Some individuals emerge from this childhood experience with unappeased and unappeasable needs for affect; others with a submissiveness acquired in coping with adult wills; and all with enough residue of both to give rise to a widespread empathetic understanding of domination itself, and of the needs it satisfies from above and from below.

Infancy is thus the great readying experience that prepares us for the adult condition of sub- and superordination—an experience that appears so "natural" that few inquire as to the origin or nature of the desire to impose one's will, or the pleasure that is derived from its imposition, or the obverse, the impulse to acquiesce in, or even to identify sympathetically with, the imposition of another's will over oneself. Infancy is the condition from which we must all escape, and as such, the source of the emancipatory thrust that is also part of the human drama; but it is as well a condition to which we all to some degree wish to return, the prototype of the existential security that we also seek.*

These roots of the power relation in human infancy do not, however, explain a crucial aspect of domination as an historic fact. It is that organized power is not a universal aspect of human history but a condition that only appeared when the first states arose from the aboriginal social formation of humankind. Thus the elements of the unconscious from which the act of domination draws its attraction, both for those who seek it and for those who yield to it, supply a necessary basis for understanding the psychological functions of power, but they do not sufficiently explain why humankind throughout the world took the extraordinary step of abandoning an equality of access to resources to enter into a condition in which the great majority of individuals became more or less permanently dependent on a small minority.

Only conjectures can fill this gap in our knowledge. Given the weakness of the power accorded prestigious

---

*The domination by men of women, a profound shaping element in social history, undoubtedly requires a different analysis from that of the domination of social classes. Nonetheless, the pleasures of male superincumbency and the appeals of female submission must be explained, not explained away by assuming that domination is intrinsically pleasurable and submission painful. I would think the same general aspects of the human psyche would apply to the case of patriarchy as to that of class rule.

individuals in primitive societies, and the tendency of these groups to fragment into smaller bands once the threshold of a dangerous infringement on independence is reached, it seems reasonable to assume that external pressures of some kind—limitations (or unusual concentrations) of resources, or the gradual forces of population growth, or the perceived advantages of a social division of labor—may have pushed self-sufficient communities into social differentiations, distinctions of rank, stratification, and finally differential access to resources. That this process must at some stage have required force rather than drift is evidenced by the universal "legitimation" of property rights by military power.[11]

Whatever its origins, the organized state, once established, had little difficulty in extending its dominion over unorganized communities. The advantages of a superior class or group that could marshall the labor of the underlying population were quickly apparent in the pursuit of war and in the accumulation of surplus. Following a theme of German historiography, the historian Alexander Rustow offers this plausible, if perhaps fanciful, reconstruction of a neolithic push of horsed nomads into the territories of sedentary cultivators, perhaps as a consequence of climatic displacement:

The rider appears on the stage of history like a new breed of man, marked by a powerful superiority; he is over two meters in height and moves several times faster than a pedestrian. The enormous impact that the first of such riders must have made

---

11. See Fried, *Evolution of Political Society,* pp. 183f., 230; also H. Claessen and P. Skalnik, eds., *The Early State,* (The Hague: Mouton Publishers, 1978), esp. Ch. 2, Ronald Cohen, "State Origins: A Reappraisal."

on peaceful stockbreeders is depicted in the legendary form of the centaur. . . .

Superincumbency brought victors and vanquished, as upper and lower strata, into opposing social situations that would eventually produce equally diverse effects in selection, breeding, and hereditary character traits. The upper stratum was trained to cultivate lust for power, arrogance, pride, a sense of superiority, toughness, cruelty, and sadism, for the more it possessed and practiced these characteristics, the more solidly it sat in the saddle of superstratification. The corresponding characteristics of the lower stratum were subservience, flexibility, submissiveness, servility, spinelessness, masochism—for the more it possessed and practiced these characteristics the better it adapted itself to the role assigned by fate.[12]

Thus there is no difficulty in explaining how power, once set into place, could expand its domain and reinforce its own structure. The aspect of domination that requires elucidation, we repeat, appears so self-evident as to be in danger of being left unexplained. This is the characteristic of human nature that opens the possibility of a structure of domination in the first place, the aggressive and passive elements in the unconscious without which the exercise or sufferance of power could not originally appear.

As we shall see in our next chapter, there are important considerations introduced into the mechanism of power once it is exercised through the accumulation of capital, including the quality of insatiability that is an inherent aspect of the drive to amass power-as-capital, whereas an insatiable drive after power in other guises appears only as

---

12. A. Rustow, *Freedom and Domination* (Princeton, N.J.: Princeton University Press, trans. 1980), pp. 29, 47.

a pathology. As Marx was to say in a somewhat different context, "while the miser is merely a capitalist gone mad, the capitalist is a rational miser."[13] Indeed we will see that the very absence of direct coercion in the social relationship of capital introduces an element of necessitous expansion that is largely missing from the exercise of power in other ways.

At the moment, however, it is enough to recognize that the drive to amass wealth is inextricable from power, and incomprehensible except as a form of power. The social formation of capitalism must therefore be seen in the first instance as a *regime* comparable to regimes of military force, religious conviction, imperial beliefs, and the like. Capitalism is the regime of capital, the form of rulership we find when power takes the remarkable aspect of the domination, by those who control access to the means of production, of the great majority who must gain "employment"—the capitalist substitute for the traditional entitlement of the peasant to consume some portion of his own crop.

---

13. Karl Marx, *Capital,* I (New York: Vintage Books, 1977) p. 254.

# 3

# The Regime of Capital

WE HAVE COME to the point when we can describe capitalism as a stratified society in which the accumulation of wealth fulfills two functions: the realization of prestige, with its freight of unconscious sexual and emotional needs, and the expression of power, with its own constellation of unconscious requirements and origins. When Marx calls capital "self-expanding value" he is underscoring the function of capital as an embodiment of power, for the essence of capital to Marx is its domination over labor; but when Veblen stresses the emulatory behavior to which capital gives rise, he is explicitly stressing the resemblances between the symbolic properties of capital as wealth and the prestige objects of primitive societies. Both aspects of capital can be seen in capitalist social formations, where the process of accumulating capital is pursued in part because it is the manner in which the dominant class expresses and renews its social control and in part because it is the typical means by which preeminence and distinction is achieved in the socioeconomic world.

The sublimation of the drive for power into the drive for capital not only demarcates the nature of the system—that is, its behavior-shaping properties—but also affects its logic, the movement that emerges from the social formation. We have already noted a number of such distinctive traits, but we must now inquire more deeply into a few of them. One aspect is the insatiability that characterizes the process of capital, endlessly converting money into commodities and commodities into money. There is no exact parallel for this in other manifestations of power. Megalomania and narcissism are motivational elements in all systems, but in none is the normal reach of power so nakedly unbounded in aim.

The "rational miser" who personifies the capitalist for Marx must therefore find in the circuits of capital both the means and the motive to pursue an endless quest for aggrandizement—a quest so patently without rationality, and so perilously liable to bring psychological discontent, that Adam Smith was forced to find its rationalization in a delusion imposed upon us by the Deity. "Power and riches," he wrote, " . . . [are] . . . enormous and operose machines contrived to produce a few trifling conveniencies to the body . . . which, in spite of all our care, are ready every moment to burst into pieces, and to crush in their ruins their unfortunate possessor." And yet, Smith goes on, "it is well that nature imposes upon us in this manner. It is this deception which rouses and keeps in continual motion the industry of mankind." There follows almost immediately the first reference to the Invisible Hand, Smith's immortal designation of the benign outcome imposed on unknowing humans by a beneficent deity.[1]

---

1. Adam Smith, *Theory of Moral Sentiments,* pp. 182–83.

We can find a more compelling explanation for the drive to amass capital by looking further into the very attribute of capital to which we initially turned our attention—namely, the generality of its wealth-form compared with the specific use values in which wealth is embodied in pre-capitalist systems. The result of this generalization of wealth is that comparisons and calculations impossible in such societies become not only possible but imperative. Capital reduces all forms of wealth, whether sought for prestige or power, to money terms, and this common basis of measurement now brings far-reaching changes in the behavioral dispositions of individuals who seek wealth.

When wealth is realized in objects that directly embody prestige or power, there is no objective means of measuring the amount of personal or social enhancement represented by any given element of riches. But under the regime of capital a strict calculus emerges with respect to prestige or power—namely, the extent of money capital. Moreover, by its very abstract nature there are no bounds imposed on the size of the wealth by which power and prestige are symbolized, in contrast to the limitations often imposed by the sheer physical bulk of material riches. Thus the very abstract nature of economic life under capitalism—the severance of the daily round from the hand of tradition and custom and its deliverance to the aegis of economic plus and minus—serves a twofold purpose. As Max Weber and others have emphasized, it introduces into capitalism a prevailing "rationality" of conduct, a consideration of means and ends, a supersession of unruly passions by calculating interests. Further, by discovering in all objects—indeed in nearly all activities—an abstract dimension of money equivalances, it insinuates a limitlessness into the calculation of wealth that Aristotle was the first to perceive and fear.[2]

To the imagination-freeing properties of the abstract aspect of money capital must be added a second attribute that also spurs on the endless effort to accumulate. This arises because capital, unlike the use values that embody prestige and power in tributary systems, exists in a constant state of vulnerability as it passes through its neverending circuits of M-C-M'.

The vulnerability results from the continuous dissolution of objects into money, which returns all embodiments of wealth to a common reservoir accessible to all other capitalists. Objects of prestige or coercive power—gold or arms, for instance—may be exposed to seizure or to loss for other reasons, but they are not, as part of their intrinsic being, regularly dissolved into another form that is available to any rival. But that is precisely what the circuit of capital imposes on its possessors. Capital is powerful only insofar as it continuously runs the gauntlet of circulation, each capitalist of necessity distributing his money into the hands of the public (his workers, his suppliers) in order to procure the labor services and materials from which his capital will be reconstituted as a commodity. Each capitalist must win back from the public at large the money capital he has disbursed to various sections of it, and each capitalist is simultaneously trying to win for himself as much as possible of the money capital of other capitalists

---

2. See Max Weber, *The Protestant Ethic* (London: Allen and Unwin, 1976); for "interests" see Albert Hirschmann, *The Passions and the Interests* (Princeton, N.J.: Princeton University Press, 1977); Aristotle, *Politics,* Book I.

that has been relinquished in similar fashion.

*This continuous dissolution and recapture is the essence of the process of competition,* which can now be seen as an element in the working of the system that directly stems from the nature of capital itself. Competition does not simply mean the vying of vendors who sell similar products in a market, which is the way contemporary economics perceives it, but the inescapable exposure of each capitalist to the efforts of others to gain as much as possible of the public's purchasing power. Competition therefore has little to do with prestige, despite its surface aspects of vying, and it is not directly connected with the exercise of domination, because competition does not immediately pit capitalists against workers but capitalists against other capitalists. Rather, competition is the instantiation in the economic world of that "warre of each against all" that Hobbes imagined to be the original and always latent condition of the political world. In Hobbes's world, protection against the threat of mutual devastation was gained by the delegation of power to Leviathan, the state, in the form of a social contract; but in the economic war among capitalists no such protection is possible because, as we shall see later, the very creation of the realm of capital requires the exclusion of Leviathan's power from its domain. The state can buffer competition in individual markets, but it cannot call off the "warre of each against all" that results from the M-C-M' circuit.

Thus capital itself introduces a form of social war; and social war brings a new intensity to the drive for wealth in the substratum of behavior that I am calling human nature. That new intensity derives from the motive of self-preservation, by popular repute the most intense and unrestrained of all instinctual responses. In tributary societies this motive undoubtedly also supplies some of the energy behind the accumulation of wealth, especially in response to threats from hostile kingdoms without. But only under capitalism does the threat exist within the kingdom itself, as the consequence of the naked exposure of capital during its circuitous transubstantiations.

The motive of self-preservation is therefore added to those that underpin the desire for prestige and for power. As before, however, we must distinguish between the animal and the human significance of the "motive" of self-preservation. Among animals, self-preservation is a response mobilized by a threat to existence, but in the social world—especially that of economic competition—the threat is not that of death but of social diminution. Competition is more likely to be a literal matter of self-preservation when it takes place among the bottom stratum of the working class, especially in early capitalism, than among capitalists. Thus the additional stimulus given to the drive for wealth by its generalization as capital does not supplant its unconscious meanings of personal preeminence and social domination but sharpens and intensifies the energies that must be devoted to its protection and to its accumulation.

Because of its necessitous exposure to capture, however, the defense of capital cannot be mounted like that of a citadel. On the contrary, the only defense available to any capitalist, large or small, is an unrelenting concentration on the successful recapture of capital-as-money from the hands of the public. Here is the root of the acquisitive behavior of the business world that we can now see as a necessary expression of the nature of capital itself.

The acquisitive orientation has two aspects. One of them is the aggressive attitude of participants in the economic sphere with respect to money-making itself. The need continuously to recapture capital from its dissolved form encourages—indeed, requires—an antagonistic stance toward the other participants in the market process. Thus arises the often-noticed difference between the attitudes of members of market societies and those of nonmarket societies—the former reducing human contact in order to minimize the emotional entanglements that might interfere with the necessary stance of impersonal acquisitiveness; the latter freely expressing personal interaction on the local marketplace, because an unremitting orientation toward the expansion of money wealth has not become an integral part of the social process.

A second aspect of the acquisitive orientation involves the encouragement given to protective maneuvers. One of these, to which we will return in our next chapter, concerns the use of the powers of the state to limit the dangers of the mutual encroachment of capitals. As we will see, this has only limited possibilities. The other, of profound importance, is the use of all available means to gain a competitive advantage over other capitals. By far the most effective of these means is the development of new modes of organizing the M-C-M′ circuit in its middle link. By changing the manner in which commodities are gathered or made, it is possible to increase the likelihood of gathering M′, whether because the new method of dealing with the commodity link is more efficient or because the commodity itself is novel or newly designed. In a word, each capitalist to some extent commands control over the technology that fashions the commodity by which M' must be recaptured, so that the systematic encouragement and development of technological capabilities of all kinds become an integral consequence of the M-C-M' sequence itself.

In turn this brings an implosive aspect to the expansion of capital, as daily life is scanned for possibilities that can be brought within the circuit of accumulation. The transformation of activities that bring pleasure- or use-values into activities that also yield a profit to their organizers thus becomes an important "interior" realm into which capital expands. The steady movement of such tasks as laundering, cooking, cleaning, and simple health care—not to mention recreation and entertainment—from the exclusive concern of the private household into the world of business testifies to the internal expansion of capital within the interstices of social life. Much of what is called "growth" in capitalist societies consists in this commodification of life, rather than in the augmentation of unchanged, or even improved, outputs. The continuous emphasis on "time-saving" inventions or the unrelenting efforts of business to induce individuals to adopt new life styles are instances of this commodifying aspect of the self-expanding property of capital.

## II

The expansive nature of capital affects its systemic motion—its logic—in yet one more important way. It is the source of a general disciplinary pressure that, together with the thrust of the acquisitive impulse itself, establishes the self-ordering tendency that is one of the general characteristics of capitalism. That is, the configurational path traced by the system, both in terms of its rhythms of expansion and its patterns of organization, is in large part the consequence of the expansion and collision of its units of business that we now perceive as an aspect of the nature of capital.

The specific character and outcome of this interaction of expansive units of capital hinges on many elements in the institutional structure of the system, including its technical apparatus, its prevailing business and cultural ethos, and its ideology of government, so that competition has different forms and consequences for a world of small-scale capitals—to use Adam Smith's word—than it does for one of giant capitals. We will look more carefully into some of these problems in Chapter 6 when we examine the general logic of the system. But at this juncture we still need to delve further into the disciplinary force itself—the general magnetic pull, to revert to our metaphor, that is generated by the mutual encroachment of the M-C-M' circuits.

Here we can distinguish two widespread effects. The first of these is the subordination of the capitalists' efforts to obtain wealth to the objective requirements of "the market"—that is, to the purchases of usually unknown buyers. We have already noted the process of commodification by which the capitalist seeks to widen his market. Whether created by his own efforts or not, however, it is the needs or desires of the public, not those of the accumulator, that must be satisfied in order to gain wealth. The drive for wealth is thereby tied into the production of use-values—not as the embodiment or "end" of wealth-seeking, but as the vehicle, the means, by which it is realized. This is, of course, Smith's invisible hand—the historic apologia for capitalism, uncontestable insofar as it emphasizes the necessity of the system to cater to the material appetites of its population; uneasy when asked to account for the origins or characteristics of these appetites and their congruence with the moral development of society.[3]

The subordination of the search for capital to the requirements of the market is evidenced not only in the piling up of social wealth but in the general necessity of capitalists to abide by socially imposed limits on the accumulation process. The level of wages or rents or interest that the capitalist must pay, no less than the rate of profit he can expect, is also set by "the market," and further reflects the inability of the capitalist to coerce his suppliers of services or his buyers of output. Thus in the idealized representation of capitalism as "economics," the capitalist becomes a personage without any power whatsoever, forced to accept the costs and the price levels imposed by market processes over which he has no control.

Apparently powerless "capitals" thereby provide the basis for the self-correcting logic of the system. The accumulative momentum is constantly held in check by the

---

3. There is a considerable literature on this moral contradiction, of which two influential examples are R. H. Tawney, *The Acquisitive Society* (New York: Harcourt, Brace & Co., 1948) and John Kenneth Galbraith, *The Affluent Society* (Boston: Houghton Mifflin, 1958).

pressures of "the market," and its path of productive output constantly tracks the wants and needs of consumers. Later we shall look more critically into this conception of economic order and growth, but for the moment it presents accurately enough the manner in which the system generates a disciplinary force over its own workings.

A second disciplinary force emerges as the maximizing drive of capital becomes generalized throughout all strata of society. We have seen that the rise of capital as a relation of domination has as its necessary precondition the existence of a class of agricultural and urban workers who no longer have direct rights of access to the productive equipment and resources of society. They are thereby made dependent for their livelihoods on their ability to survive in a market milieu where access to livelihood requires the acceptance of prevailing rates of pay, and in which the need to secure employment instills a competitive point of view with respect to earnings in contrast to the traditional and customary approach of premarket societies.

This enforced competitiveness allows the same description of "maximizing behavior" to be applied to the worker as to the capitalist, despite the polarity of their existential positions in terms of power. As a consequence, a similar behavioral propensity is instilled in workers and capitalists alike, both engaged in an struggle to gain access to society's money wealth and both constrained by the mutual encroachment of others engaged in the same pursuit. Not only are the two sides thereby exposed to the dictates of the market, which forces its participants to act from the same motives of aggressive defense, but they also begin to share motives of a different kind. The general pressures of domination remain the prerogative of the capitalist, but the lure of income as a means to the acquisition of prestige becomes a force for mobilizing workers as soon as the general wage level, or wage differentials, permit the upper tier of the work force to purchase prestige goods. Such varied observers as Tocqueville, Veblen, and Tawney have noted that the acquisitive attitudes at the apex of the pyramid rapidly percolate to the bottom, where they play their role both to reinforce the discipline of employment and to unify the social perception of the system.

The disciplinary force of competition that guides so many aspects of the logic of capitalism is also, then, rooted in its nature; and the relevant aspect of its nature in this case is the replacement of the older forms of wealth as use-values by the generalized form of wealth as capital. This is the "cash nexus" of which Marx and Engels spoke in the *Manifesto*. The all-important consequence of this diffusion of maximizing behavior is that the individual particles of capitalist society, workers as well as capitalists, become susceptible to the magnetic forces of the marketplace, following its price signals as arrows indicating the appropriate movements of their behavior as buyers or sellers. The result of this pervasive magnetization is the creation of an economic "system" that attains its coherence and continuity not from the influence of tradition pressing from below, or from command imposing its will from above, but by the unintended outcome of self-guided activities arising within.

## III

In the paradox of a system of power whose protagonists are mainly conscious of their powerlessness lies one of the most mystifying attributes of capitalism. How can the capitalist class be deemed the "ruling" class of a system when it is itself at the mercy of market forces? At the risk of repeating what is by now wearisomely familiar, the answer lies in fundamental inequalities of social position, manifested primarily in the respective capacities of different elements to supply their own livelihoods, a contrast described by Adam Smith, we recall, with his customary frankness.[4]

Because capital is the form in which power is denominated under capitalism we must now look more carefully into the relationship between the accumulation of capital and the exercise of this fundamental disparity of social position. The relationship is best examined in the locus where it is of greatest significance and of least self-evident clarity—namely, in the manner in which profits appear in the circuit of capital.

Profits take on different forms under capitalism. Initially they arise as the gains from trade made by merchants. This is not an exclusively capitalist means to profit, for merchants' gains come into being wherever the possibility exists of buying a commodity at a lower price than one can sell it for, a state of affairs as ancient as civilization (we have records of mercantile dealings from the kingdom of Sumer). The possibility of trading profits

---

4. See above, p. 41n. (Smith, *Wealth of Nations,* p. 84).

depends on unequal positions of strength, whether based on political subjugation, or on the possession of knowledge, or on a monopoly of buying or selling power enjoyed by the trader: if strength were equal on both sides of the market there is no reason why a merchant should be able to buy "cheap" or sell "dear." This form persists to this day as an extremely important form of profit in both capitalist and noncapitalist countries, not least in the relationships of inequality that allow richer countries or companies to conclude advantageous trade arrangements with poorer ones.

Of greater historical significance are the profits that arise under capitalism from the unique relationship between capital and labor—namely, as a surplus derived from the activity of production, not exchange. Here the key institution—the institution that reflects the inequality of power at the core of capitalism—is that of wage labor, the peculiar mode of allowing workers access to resources that only comes into being after the dependency of labor has been historically established. Under a wage labor system workers are entirely free to enter or leave the work relationship as they wish. They cannot be forced or dragooned into work or compelled to stay at work if they wish to quit. In the eyes of many conservative theorists, it is this contractual right of refusal—a right that protects both employer and employee from the coercive use of his property (capital in the case of the employer, the capacity to labor in that of the worker)—that constitutes the essential political foundation of capitalism and, beyond that, its essential justification as a moral order.

These freedoms are indeed of great importance, although as we shall see later, they are narrow definitions of what freedom can imply. More to the point, however, the freedom from impressment equally enjoyed by labor and capital does not betoken an equality of their respective entitlements. For the wage labor relationship includes a legal provision that is wholly at odds with the equal footing on which the owners of labor and capital apparently confront one another in the marketplace. The understanding is that the product itself belongs to the owner of the capital resources that are used in production, not to the owners of the labor resources who receive a payment—their wage—and who have no legal claim to their product.

Thus the wage relationship itself becomes a manner in which the domination of one class over another is invisibly introduced into the workings of the system. In this regard it is enlightening to reflect on the question of who can lay claim to the cars that roll off the General Motors assembly line. It is not the workers or the management: no managerial official, including the president of the company, has the legal right to claim an automobile as his own, without paying for it. Nor is it the stockholders: the largest stockholder in General Motors cannot take possession of a car without payment, simply by virtue of the ownership of shares of stock.

Who, then, owns the output? The answer is that it is owned by whoever owns the physical plant and equipment, the capital. If the company is a proprietorship, the owner has a *legal* right to what is produced and may

67

indeed claim it for private use instead of selling it. In the case of a corporation, the owner of the capital equipment is a fictitious personage, the corporation. The owner of the cars coming off GM's assembly line is therefore General Motors, a legal creature in whom is vested the ownership of the company's physical assets as well as the right of hiring its work force, from janitor to president. As the saying goes, the cars are "company property."

This relation between work and reward, in which the worker, including the most skilled and highly-paid manager, is paid for services rendered but is not entitled to lay physical or legal claim to output, comes into full-fledged existence for the first time under capitalism. No ancient society uses the wage labor relation as a principal means of gathering surplus. The peasants of antiquity are never paid wages but retain a residual right to the crops they harvest, even though a very large, often crushing fraction of those crops is taken from them as rents, tithes, or dues. Feudal serfs directly appropriate the output from their strips of land, although they are forced to hand over a share as rent, or to cultivate other strips whose product belongs entirely to the lord. Artisans have always possessed their own products, although the terms of their sale might be strictly regulated. Only the slave had no claim to his own production, whence Marx's designation of the capitalist wage relation as "wage slavery."

Before Marx, something very like this crucial relationship had already been described by John Locke. Discussing the nature of property in his *Second Treatise on Government* in 1690, Locke wrote: "The grass my horse has bit, *the turfs my servant has cut,* and the ore I have digged in any place . . . become my property without the assignation or consent of anybody."[5]

Locke's "servant" cannot be deemed a Marxian proletarian, as the servant enters into his relationship voluntarily rather than because he has no alternative. The illustration nonetheless makes vivid the tacit agreement to relinquish ownership in the fruit of one's labor that is the basis of a wage contract. In this silent clause of the contract is hidden an essential qualification of the freedom that plays so important a role in the conservative vision of capitalism. What is omitted from this vision is an explicit acknowledgment of the terms and conditions that *precede* the market encounter of worker and employer, terms and conditions that in no way diminish the legal freedom of the market bargain but that place the transaction in a very different position from that of ordinary market relationships.

How can a profit arise from wage labor? Obviously it can only come into being if the employer pays the laborer less than the value of the laborer's product. Smith and Ricardo indeed believed that the market mechanism established a wage for labor below the value of labor's output, so that a margin was made available to the capitalist: "The value *which the workmen add to the material,"*

---

5. John Locke, *Second Treatise on Government* (Boston: Beacon Press, 1975), p. 18 (my italics). See also C. B. Macpherson, *The Political Theory of Possessive Individualism* (New York: Oxford University Press, 1962) and a critique by Jas. Tully, *A Discourse on Property* (New York: Cambridge University Press, 1980).

wrote Smith, " . . . resolves itself . . . into two parts, of which the one pays their wages, the other the profits of the employer."[6]

Thus in Smith's view, the origin of profit lies in sharing the value created by labor, and the capitalist's claim to profit is his right to be recompensed for "hazarding" his stock (his capital) in the undertaking. This resembles the modern explanation of profit as the right of the capitalist to appropriate any residual, after he has paid out all wages and other costs of production including depreciation, for which he has hazarded his capital. The difference between Smith's view and that of contemporary economics is that Smith locates the original source of profits in the regular appropriation by captalists of a share of the value of the product of labor, whereas modern economics has no way of explaining why there should be any *persisting* residual to be appropriated, assuming that competition prevents capitalists from forming an economywide conspiracy or cartel.

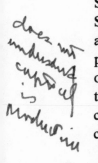

Indeed, in the classical view, the residual was constantly in peril of disappearing as the competition among employers for labor raised wages and consequently reduced the residual. Smith and Ricardo both believed that a margin of profits would only be maintained because rising wages spurred population growth, and population growth in turn depressed or retarded the increase in wages, thereby safeguarding the capitalist's "share."

Whether or not population growth is the safeguarding mechanism, it is clear that the accumulation process, to be

---

6. Smith, *Wealth of Nations,* p. 66. (my italics).

successful, requires some means of preventing wages from rising until they absorb all profits. The manner in which this possibility is avoided constitutes one of the most revealing themes of the great economic scenarios. For Smith and Ricardo, as we have just mentioned, the safeguarding mechanism is the increase in labor supply generated by wage increases themselves—higher wages allowing the poor to bring to working age a larger number of their children. For Marx the mechanism is the "overpopulation" created by the accumulation process, as capitalists not only demand more labor but also more equipment, and then use the latter to displace the former. In either case, all the great classical economists through John Stuart Mill saw higher wages as directly encroaching on profits, and they further saw the accumulation process as setting into motion the necessary social responses to ward off that eventuality. If there were no mechanism to protect the employer's share, he would simply not hire workers because, as Smith explains, "He would have no interest to employ them unless he expected from the sale of their work something more than what was sufficient to replace his stock [capital] to him."[7]

The classical conception thus located the origin of profit in the diversion of some part of the value created by the working members of society into the hands of a dominant class. There was no sense of injustice in this acknowledgment but rather the recognition of the central importance of the function of capitalism, which was to accumulate capital. Implicit in this conception, unfortunately, was the

7. Smith, *Wealth of Nations,* p. 66.

awkward conclusion that labor was nonetheless deprived of the full value of its product, part of which was appropriated by the capitalist.

Curiously, it was Marx who sought to remove the implication that profits represented only an "unfair" division of the product, through his distinction between labor as a process and labor as a commodity. Labor as a process consists in the energies and intelligence of a person engaged in production. Labor as a commodity consists of an object produced for sale—in this case, the "labor power," or working capacity of a laborer. The normal market price of the commodity labor power is a wage that will permit the commodity to be regularly produced—that is, a wage sufficient to allow the worker who owns and sells his working capacity on the market to purchase a conventional standard of living. In the wage-labor relationship, competition among employers forces them to pay such a conventional wage, but the wage relationship entitles them in return to the actual labor—the expenditure of energy—that the laborer can perform in a normal working day. The source of surplus then resides in the presence of a regularly recurring margin between the market value of the commodities the worker will produce during the working day and the wages needed to maintain the labor power of the worker, plus the costs of whatever capital goods or intermediate materials are used up in the process of production.

The margin is Marx's famous "surplus value"—the unpaid labor that accrues to the capitalist by virtue of his position of dominance in the wage labor engagement. From this hidden source of value Marx can now expand his M-C-M' formula—from a money sum to a larger money sum—into the form M-C-C-M', to denote the critical source of profit *within* the production process itself, symbolized by the increase in the value of C to C'; and from the deeper implications of surplus value he derives the scenario of a system driven by the complex laws of motion that arise from the constant need to create surplus value or to protect it against forces that tend to erode it.*

Finally, we must consider a mode of profit extraction that appears with increasing visibility in modern capitalism. This is technological innovation. When innovation takes the form of a new product, the capitalist enjoys a monopolistic profit, often of short-lived duration, and reaps a surplus from society in essentially the same fashion as the trader who possesses scarce and desired goods. When technological advance lowers costs of production, the pioneering capitalist enjoys an advantage analogous to that of a fortunately situated, low-cost landlord.

Conventional analysis treats these technologically derived "rents" as a source of profit different from that of trade or production and designates them as "Schumpeterian" profits, after their most influential expositor.[8] Marxian analysis, which traces all profit from production to surplus value, treats technological rents as Marx treated

---

*The conception of surplus value rooted in production is distinct from the labor theory of value, which is an attempt to explain relative prices in terms of labor power. Wage labor can produce a surplus, whatever the source of value, as long as the price of labor power plus used-up materials is less that the price of labor's product.

8. Joseph Schumpeter, *The Theory of Economic Development* (Cambridge, Mass.: Harvard University Press, 1979), Ch. 4; also *Business Cycles* (New York: McGraw-Hill, 1939), Ch. III.

land rents, namely as a transfer of part of the total surplus value generated within production from less strategically placed capitalists to more strategically located ones.

We do not have to weigh the merits of the conventional and Marxian views in this matter. What is crucial is that technological rents, like profits obtained through trade or the direct exploitation of labor, owe their existence to the system of property rights on which capitalism is erected. That is, however profits may appear under capitalism—as trading gains, sweated labor, monopolistic advantage, or differences in cost—they become manifest as "residuals" *that are deemed to belong to the owners of capital, not to the owners of labor power.* The economic category of profits is thereby revealed to be a disguised form of the fundamental dominative basis of the system, into whose social and psychological roots we have already inquired.

This consideration of the nature of profits allows us to take up the crucial idea of *exploitation,* a term inseparable from any discussion of wealth or power. Exploitation carries pejorative connotations that, however justified, may obscure an understanding of the issue. The essential meaning of exploitation is that a surplus is seized from the working population for the benefit of a superior class. Such a seizure will be exploitative even if the surplus yields social benefits at large, in addition to the power or prestige for which it was originally brought into being, as in the case of Roman roads, Christian churches, or the factories of capitalism. It is this *class* orientation of surplus that provides the analytic as well as the moral core of the problem: "The surplus . . . whether small or great, is usually torn from the producers, either by the government to which they are subject, or by individuals, who by superior force, or by availing themselves of religious or traditional feelings of subordination, have established themselves as lords of the soil." It is not Marx speaking but John Stuart Mill.[9]

To the extent that modern-day capitalist profits stem from technological rents, the exploitation of labor becomes increasingly difficult to identify as visibly overworked or underpaid workers. As we have seen, however, exploitation has a characteristic of class disposition as well as class seizure. What counts is not merely the means of extraction of some portion of social production but the purposes to which this surplus portion is largely put. Profit, in its various forms, represents a novel means of amassing surplus, especially as surplus value or technological rent, but the flow of surplus into the hands of a dominant class is unchanged, despite the use of property rights, rather than coercion, as the means of siphoning wealth upward.

It is therefore entirely possible that the *origin* of surplus in the era of capitalism has gradually moved from trade through direct wage labor exploitation toward technological rents, and that modern-day profits consist of combinations of all three.[10] What is significant is that the *allocation*

9. John Stuart Mill, *Principles of Political Economy* (Toronto: University of Toronto Press, 1965), p. 13.

10. See Ernest Mandel, *Late Capitalism* (London: New Left Books, 1975), Ch. 3.

of this surplus to the capital-owning class has not been affected by the alteration in its sources. In all cases surplus moves toward the apex of society, where capital ownership is concentrated. In various stages of capitalism this surplus is explained as deriving from the skill of the merchant, the risk-bearing function of capitalists, the productivity of capital goods, or the power of technology. These explanations, however, only describe the strategic means by which the fundamental power of capital is applied. That fundamental power lies in the right of owners of wealth to withhold it from use unless they are permitted to appropriate whatever trading gains or surplus values or technological rents or risk-bearing rewards appear when capital is placed at the disposal of society.

Thus we can see that the winning of profit in any form represents the successful exercise of a basically political relationship. Profit is the life blood of capitalism, not merely because it is the means by which individual capitals obtain their wherewithal for expansion but because it is the manner in which the relation of domination is evidenced. The continuous generation of profits generates its euphoric atmosphere because it gives evidence that the regime is fulfilling its political mission—namely, organizing society according to the principles and ends for which it exists. Profits are for capitalism the functional equivalent of the acquisition of territory or plunder for military regimes, or an increase in the number of believers for religious ones, or the legitimation of recognized authority for states in which a change of rulership has taken place. They are the concrete representation of the intangible structure of power, hierarchy, privilege, and belief that arise from the system's nature and that give rise to its logic. In all depictions of the business system profits are the key economic variable, but in any depiction of the regime of capitalism they must be the parameters of its central historical task.

# 4

# The Role of the State

UNTIL NOW we have spoken of capitalism mainly in terms of the elements that explain and shape behavior in the marketplace—the imperative search for capital, the mutual encroachment of capitals, the "maximizing" activity that is reflected in the ebb and flow of market supply and demand. Behind these market forces lie other, sometimes even more significant, levels of change that also emanate from the nature of the system— the constant reorganization of work skills and work organization, of managerial structures, of technical equipment, all governed by the effort to accumulate capital as effectively as possible. What we have called the scenarios of capitalism are the stylized accounts of these induced movements—the ascending, undulating profile of total output, the evolving arrangements of men and machines in typical factory and office centers, the changing size and structure of the administrative framework that operates each unit of capital.

In Chapter 6 we will look further into some of these idealized narratives, but we have not yet sufficiently examined the essential elements of the socioeconomic formation itself. For capitalism cannot be understood in terms of its structure of production alone, any more than tributary states can be grasped exclusively in political, or primitive societies in communal, terms. Social formations combine aspects of all these facets to create mutually supportive (and sometimes contradictory) totalities; and an attempt to describe the nature and logic of any formation by paying heed only to that aspect that is most immediately visible or active risks the distortions of reductionism, whatever the basis to which the analysis is reduced.

At the same time, like all social formations, capitalism is not merely a Chinese puzzle in which all elements are of equal importance in locking together the whole. In capitalism as in other regimes, a central organizing principle and its institutions influence all aspects of the social formation, whether these be concerned with material life, justice and social order, or custom and belief. In primitive societies that organizing principle is kinship with its networks of reciprocity; in tributary societies it is the principle of centralized rulership with its associated aristocratic or priestly hierarchies; and in capitalism, as we have so often discussed, it is capital with its self-expanding attributes.

In insisting on the pervasive importance of identifying historically specific cores within social formations, I am very much aware of the pitfalls of reductionism, against which I have just warned the reader. These dangers, mordantly described by E. P. Thompson, derive from a mechanical conception of social relations in which rigid determinations force all elements in society to respond in mechanical fashion to changes in the foundational structure.[1] As I shall attempt to demonstrate in the pages that follow, this impoverishment of social analysis is by no means an unavoidable consequence of the central placement of a given set of institutions with their attendant belief systems. Rather, the sense of an historical reference point implicit in such a central placement gets us around the difficulties that arise from a failure to assign any hierarchy of importance to principles, so that society does indeed take on the appearance of a Chinese puzzle without a decisive structural element.

Let me instance this difficulty in a work in which I find much to admire, *The Cultural Contradictions of Capitalism* by Daniel Bell.[2] Bell, like Braudel, avoids defining the concept of capitalism despite its prominence in the title of his work. Instead he describes "modern society" as the product of a "disjunction" of realms, no one of which clearly dominates the whole. He writes:

> . . . I find it more useful to think of *contemporary* society . . . as three distinct realms, each of which is obedient to a different axial principle. I divide society, analytically, into the *techno-economic* structure, the *polity,* and the *culture.* These are not congruent with one another and have different rhythms of change; they follow different norms which legitimate different, and even contrasting, types of behavior. It is the discordances between these realms which are responsible for the various contradictions within society.[3]

---

1. See E. P. Thompson, *The Poverty of Theory* (New York: Monthly Review Press, 1978), Ch. 1.

2. Daniel Bell, *The Cultural Contradictions of Capitalism* (New York: Basic Books, 1976). See also his *The Winding Passage* (Cambridge, Mass.: Abt Books, 1980), pp. xiv–xv.

3. Bell, *Cultural Contradictions,* p. 10 (his italics).

Bell's focus on distinct economic, political, and cultural realms would seem to bring his analysis close to mine. There is, however, a sharp difference. Take, for instance, the techno-economic structure. As Bell describes it, this realm "frames the occupation and stratification system of the society and involves the use of technology for instrumental ends. In modern society the axial principle is *functional rationality,* and the regulative mode is *economizing.* [4]

But what is functional rationality? Surely the answer can only be given by reference to some other underlying principle of the society. Under capitalism what criteria of "functional rationality" determine the "economizing" of labor, other than the maximization of profit? Certainly if the frame of reference was not the accumulation of capital but the development of functional or rational individuals in the sense of versatile or educated men and women, the mode of economizing accepted by the existing order would not pass muster.

In similar fashion, we discover that the principles described by Bell as "axial" in other spheres also beg the question of the referential point. In the political realm Bell designates "legitimacy" and "representation or participation" as the crucial validating concepts. In the realm of culture it is the "expression and remaking of the 'self' in order to achieve self-realization and fulfillment."[5] But as with the techno-economic sphere, these descriptions leave unasked the crucial questions: Legitimacy of what? Participation or representation in which processes?

---

4. Ibid., p. 11.
5. Bell, *Cultural Contradictions,* pp. 12, 13.

The "self" conceived as what manner of being?

What seems fatally missing from the analysis is that all of these questions are normally answered within "contemporary society" in ways that are defined by, or at least compatible with, the regime of capital. The boundaries of the terms *legitimacy, representation and participation,* and *self-expression* are conventionally decided in political life by the necessity to preserve the critical wage labor institution and to continue the generation of surplus for surplus's sake. Is this not the principle that sets the limits to "practical" politics, draws the line as to the agenda of national discussion, and validates the prevailing commercial tone of culture? Thus it is not the free contention of realms that holds the essence of capitalism, as I see it, but their tense containment within the set of economic imperatives that I have described.

A second objection to the multi-axial principle brings us to examine the purpose for which it was originally intended—namely, to provide an explanation of the corrosive, possibly fatal "contradictions" of contemporary society. The question is this: If the realms coexist in an unordered, equi-valent manner, how shall we distinguish the trials and tribulations of modern capitalism from those of other societies in the throes of their contradictions? Did not the Roman empire or late feudalism or Ming China have their techno-economic structures, their polities and their cultures, each with its axial principle? Were not the conflicts and contradictions among those realms decisive in changing, perhaps even in destroying, these societies? If that is granted, in what way are the contradictions of modern society different from those of previous ones?

The answer—and I think it is an answer with which Bell would agree—is that the contradictions of capitalism somehow arise from the nature and logic of the system— that is, from the unfolding of a society under the peculiar stresses and strains generated by its historically unique search for generalized surplus. The contradictions of other societies arose from different sources—sometimes economic; that is, rooted in the organization of labor and in the wrenching of surplus from labor's product—but equally or more frequently from political or cultural crises, such as breakdowns in political succession or religious convulsions. Contemporary society is not spared these ancient sources of disruption, but it bears within itself the seeds of another kind of endemic econonomic crisis for which no parallel can be discerned in prior social entities. This unique kind of crisis does not arise from a general disjunction of realms but from the specific tendencies of capital itself, the distinctive aspect of the society whose nature we are trying to understand.

Thus it seems to me that the failure to accord centrality to one principle and its embodying institutions—not, of course, the same ones for all social formations—robs social analysis of its clarificatory potential as gravely as the dogmatic insistence that all attributes of any given society can be explained as mere epiphenomena of its mode of production or of any other organizing structure. In our own case, unless we place the regime of capital at the center of the stage, where it dominates the play, there is no "capitalism" whose cultural contradictions have any special character. I repeat that domination is not rigid determination. There have been critical moments in the history of capitalism, as in that of other societies, when decisive blows have descended from unexpected actors, ideas, interests, or accidents. Even then, the milieu into which these blows descend, whatever their explosive power, is not a drama of Pirandello-like characters in search of identities and meanings, but a society engaged in, and enthralled by the nature, and the consequent logic, of its organizing principle.

From this perspective it is a matter of course that capital, as the dominating principle of the society identified by its presence, must color and infiltrate the institutions and beliefs that lie beyond its immediate ambit of operation. The state that carries on the formal tasks of government, or the ideational structures that contain and convey its world views, could no more escape being recognizable as "capitalist" than could the governing institutions or the ideational creations of earlier formations escape being identifiable as belonging to tributary or feudal forms of historical society. The influence of the economic realm on its intertwined political and social realms does not therefore involve any mechanical dependency or slavish passivity of the latter but only their congruence with, and complementarity to, the operating relationships of capital. Such a view is perfectly compatible with the obvious fact that the hand of the state, although generally exercised on behalf of the regime of capital, is also stayed by notions of fairness and justice, as well as political expediency. By utilizing its power to the hilt, for example, it might be possible for the state to depress wages dramatically, thereby assisting the accumulation of capital, but the full force of state power is normally held back by considerations of bourgeois morality itself, or simply by the calculations of prudence.

It is therefore not only possible, but necessary, to accord to the political and ideological realms a degree of freedom to act on behalf of motives that antedate those of capital accumulation and that persist alongside it, although generally subordinated to it. What is needed is no more—and of greater importance, no less—than a recognition of the existence of general priorities and interests without which no social formation has any historical center of gravity.

## II

I will return to the question of the permeation of the principle of capital into the other realms of its regime, partly in this chapter, partly in the next. First, however, we must look more carefully into the properties of the economic and political spheres themselves, in particular those that comprise the productive and distributive activities of the social formation, and those that define the realm charged with governance.

We have already referred to the familiar fact that no clear-cut division exists between economic and political activities in precapitalist orders. More precisely, nothing like an economic "realm" can be discovered in any of them. Of course, the physical and social undertakings necessary for material survival are visible in all societies, as are also the technical and organizational problems of altering or channeling these undertakings. What prevents these activities from constituting a "realm" is the absence of any formal boundaries that exclude the exercise of state power over the organization or direction of production or distribution. The economic domain is simply of one piece with the political. To put it somewhat differently, the crucial relationship of domination in tributary systems is applied alike with regard to the allocation of labor or the administration of justice, to the extraction of rents or the inflicting of punishment. There is no essential difference between the disciplining or the marshaling of a labor force and an army, although the former generally requires less effort because it can rely on the inertia of tradition.

As a consequence, in all tributary systems there is but one realm, that of the "political" order. I place the word in quotation marks because in many of these early systems even this aspect of domination has not acquired a distinctive association with "the state" and its apparatus, as opposed to the mere expression of a single ruler's will. What is important is that the exercise of power, whether expressed by a single ruler or a state bureaucracy, combines the enforcement of political relations of sub- and superordination with the economic performance of various tasks. Thus the warlord collecting his tribute, part of which will be conveyed to the imperium, is at one and the same time manifesting a political relationship of domination and obedience, and carrying out an economic function of surplus collection and distribution. In the same fashion, the peasant making his rental payments or taking part in a corvée is simultaneously evidencing the relationship of explicit obedience on which the polity is founded and producing the subsistence and surplus on which it lives. It is but a slight exaggeration, if any at all, to claim that there is no activity that results in the production or the allocation of material wealth that is not also the embodiment of the hierarchical principle of the system.

For an economic realm to emerge, that pervasive and unchallenged rulership must yield up some portion of its sovereignty, recognizing, so to speak, the existence of an autonomous republic of commerce and production within its own territory (and even stretching beyond it). As we know, this momentous internal secession was the consequence of the political fragmentation that followed the collapse of the Roman empire. Beginning as early as the tenth century, the mercantile estate found the protective shelter it needed in the rubble of fiefdoms that emerged from that enormous collapse. Very gradually, there arose from the widening importance of mercantile dealings, and from the increasing dependence of all levels of society on the market mechanism, the foundations of a regime of capital itself. On the land, surplus continued to be gathered through the lord's political domination over the serf, but in the towns and cities, surplus more and more welled up in the form of profits accruing to merchant traders, later in merchant guilds. Guildsmen who constituted briefly a kind of open society of independent producers in the twelfth century were the rich masters of many trades, and the dominant group in all cities, by the sixteenth century. Thus even before capitalism emerged in full dress, the appearance of a world of business presaged its entrance within late feudal Europe.

As mentioned earlier, Samir Amin has coined the term "incomplete tributary societies" to describe feudalism. The term suggests that the logic of feudalism was to remedy its incompletion by seeking self-sufficiency through military and dynastic struggles and alliances. Out of this

unstable milieu—there were some 500 more or less autonomous political units in Europe in 1500—there emerged
the cluster of strong military-administrative units that
would reduce the political crazy-quilt to a mere twenty-
five members by the year 1900.[6] The mercantile world
itself, it should be noted, experienced the same unifying
pressures that brought about the forced agglomeration of
petty fiefdoms into kingdoms, so that the petty merchant-
doms of the twelfth century grew by the fifteenth century
into the vast operations of the Bardi and Peruzzi and
Medici and the merchant bankers of Augsburg, then
into the East India Companies, the Turkey Company,
and the global commercial operations of the eighteenth
century.

From the viewpoint of the formation of two realms of
society, we see with increasing clarity the appearance of
two interdependent and yet rivalrous structures within
this extended period. One of these structures retained the
ancient trappings and much of the military power of the
original imperium and was vested with the formal respon-
sibility of enforcing the will of the state, both through its
monopoly of legal violence and its position of moral authority. At a crucial point in the seventeenth and eighteenth centuries this public realm also assumed a command
function to force modernization upon the still timid economic sphere—Colbert and Frederick the Great as exem-
plars of this early *dirigisme*. To the economic sphere itself,
without any formal recognition of the fact, was consigned
the task of superintending the daily work of the popula-

---

6. Cited in Anthony Giddens, *A Contemporary Critique of Historical Materialism* (Berkeley, Calif.: University of California Press, 1981), p. 187.

tion and of amassing the surplus of which the state itself was a main beneficiary.

The emergence of an autonomous economic realm had two aspects. One was the long and tortuous achievement of political rights for the bourgeoisie. This did not run its course until the late eighteenth century, when the full foundation was laid for a regime of capital—namely, the recognition of clear "constitutional" constraints on the power of the state to violate the private space of the individual or to commandeer his or her property. This principle of de jure equality, with its closely associated right of "private" property, formed the basis of the liberal polity. It was also this general exclusion of state power from the workings of the marketplace and from the accumulation process that prevented the state—and that still prevents it —from being able to control, other than superficially, the competitive pressures resulting from the mutual encroachment of capitals.

But this familiar story of political gain was matched by a less familiar one of economic loss. This was the gradual loss by the state of its rights of direct access to surplus. Save in unusual circumstances, the state lost its command over the labor or materials, or even the money, by which it traditionally assembled its secular, religious, or military might. Thus even though the state retained the ultimate weaponry of rule and the authority of awe, it became dependent on the operation of its self-created republic for the nourishment of revenues.

The power to tax may be the power to destroy, but the ability to tax presupposes the existence of a working economy. It is for this reason that the regime of capital is the dominant active influence in the normal relationship between the two realms, and it is why the state is normally its obliging servant. Self-interest, not weakness, drives the state to support and advance the accumulation of capital.

## III

What we find in capitalism, then, is a new form of regime in which the central organizing economic structure is divorced from the direct access to the means of violence that has always been the prerogative of the state. This reflects, at the level of national power, the absence of direct coercion that is also characteristic of capital's power at the work surface of society. It is hardly surprising, under these circumstances, that a tension between the remaining apparatus of state domination and the new structure of economic domination lies at the very heart of capitalism, vastly complicating the task of defining the relationship of state and economy. The older form of domination still "contains" the newer form, but imperfectly and uneasily; and the newer form imbues the older one with its historic mission and purpose—the accumulation of private wealth—but only partially and subject to exception.

At the core of this tension is a conflict between two logics of power: economic and political. We see this with particular clarity in comparing the roles of the two in controlling the international flow of surplus. The logic of capital is essentially one of the expansion of value which takes place, among other means, by the formation of what Immanuel Wallerstein describes as "chains" of commodities that link together more and more of the separate steps involved in the production of goods, commencing with the extraction of raw materials and ending with the sale of finished items.[7] These commodity chains combine small, discrete M-C-M' steps into longer strides, converting many small profits into fewer, larger ones. The chains are therefore organized according to opportunities of profit, not prerogatives or constraints of sovereignty. Often they stretch across regional, state, or even continental boundaries, as commodities make their ascent from their places of origin to those of disposition, accumulating value as they move. The logic of political power, by way of contrast, has always been concerned primarily with considerations of boundaries, not with those of the chains of production and distribution. It is the reach and limits of military and administrative power, not the possibilities of profit, that have guided the expansion of states.

In the era of tributary empires there was some clash of economic and political logics, insofar as the pursuits of merchants led them to ignore imperial boundaries in search of wealth, but the primacy of the political logic over that of economics is evident from the centripetal flow of surplus, out of provinces and distant regions into the imperial centers. Beijing as well as Persepolis, Rome as well as Thebes were sustained and adorned by politically organized flows of goods, whether or not these passed through mercantile hands. This simply followed from the absence of a societywide market network capable of exerting so vast a control function. Thus the basic command over the allocation of surplus was always an aspect of imperial

---

7. Immanuel Wallerstein, *Historical Capitalism* (London: Verso, 1983), p. 30.

control, in which trade played a supportive, not independent, role. (It is interesting, in this regard, to note that tributary states regularly used venturing merchants as emissaries of the realm.)

The development of an increasingly autonomous, self-directing economic realm, dominated at first by mercantile activity and then by industrial processes, disrupted this political logic insofar as the ascending flows of commodities, within or across national boundaries, were now subject to the directing forces of the marketplace, in addition to those of national sovereignty. If we examine the global flows of surplus in the epoch of capitalism, we continue to find a transfer of wealth from outlying and weak regions into central and powerful ones, but that which defines its concentration points is the presence of masses of capital—above all, money capital. These collection centers are also loci of political and, sometimes, although by no means always, military power—Japan and Switzerland as examples of nonmilitary nodes—but the order of priority of the two logics is reversed. The commanding influence over the flow of surplus is now exercised by the upward mounting chains of value-accumulating commodities, not by the direct control of military or state power. Indeed, the very possibility of maintaining an influential capitalist nation-state follows from the channeling of wealth along privately controlled commodity chains.

The commanding place that economic logic assumes with respect to the gathering and disposition of surplus introduces a characteristic tension into the political nature of capitalism. For neither state nor economy can exist by itself, and each is capable, by its faulty operation, of endangering the successful operation of the other. As we have said, the economic sphere is normally the source of the energy that suffuses and moves the entire formation, but the awesome potential of the means of violence that remains in the hands of the state is a permanent reminder that power is not denominated solely in terms of capital. In an age that has seen the rise of weaponry that puts to shame the workshop of Vulcan and the creation of a capacity for surveillance that dwarfs the wildest fantasies of Bentham's Pantopticon—his circular prison whose centrally located warden could spy on the doings of all its inmates—it would be the height of folly to claim that the regime of capital had freed itself entirely from the ancient prerogatives of government, in which, as Hobbes put it, "when nothing else is turned up, clubs are trumps."[8]

At the same time, under normal conditions in which the hand of the state is not forced on grounds of sovereignty or national existence, the realm of capital obeys a logic that often brings it into conflict with, or beyond the effective control of, the state. The chains of commodities, linked by transactions, follow a rationale over which the state is able to exert only a weak and generally ineffective guidance. This is because the creation of a realm of economics has as its basis the exclusion of state power from the M-C-M' process that is its engine of growth. The state can, of course, intervene to protect its domestic capitals

---

8. For surveillance, see Giddens, *Historical Materialism,* p. 169f.; Hobbes, *A Dialogue of The Common Laws,* cited in *Leviathan* (London: Oxford University Press, 1967), p. xvii.

from the incursion of foreign competition, but it cannot easily defend itself from the movement of its own capitals abroad or from the development of chains of commodity flows that bypass its national terrain.

Thus capital, which arises within the state and which exists originally only at the pleasure of the state, becomes increasingly capable of defying, or of existing "above," the state. A network of commodity flows cuts through the boundaries of national sovereignty to form a "system" that operates according to the dictates of its own logic, with less and less regard for those of politics. Such a world system came into existence originally with the rise of integrated market flows of broad dimensions in the sixteenth century —what Wallerstein has called a "world-economy"[9]—but in recent years its presence has become dramatically apparent in the emergence of supranational corporations and pools of money seemingly capable of eluding all constraints of political boundaries. In its most extreme form this has taken the shape of movements of capital to foreign locations, often in the semi-capitalist periphery, where the capital (in the form of mining or manufacturing units or repositories for money) serves not only as a link in the logic of commodity chains but as an affront to the logic of national power, which is unable to cope effectively with the goods or currency flows that are launched against it

---

9. Immanuel Wallerstein, *The Modern World-System* (New York: Academic Press, 1974 and 1980). There is now a large literature on this subject, of which I shall cite only two essays: Theda Skocpol, "Wallerstein's World Capitalist System: A Theoretical and Historical Critique," *American Journal of Sociology* 82 (1977): 1075–91 and Peter Worsley, "One World or Three? A Critique of the World-System Theory of Immanuel Wallerstein," *Socialist Register,* 1980, pp. 298–337.

from these foreign bases of its "own" capitals.

It is pointless to attempt to reduce this opposition of logics to a simple determination. Rather, it is the nature of the regime of capital that it exists in a condition of mixed independence from and dependence on the older regime of state power, perhaps marked by swings of centralized hegemony and rivalry.[10] That does not prevent the central organizing institution of capital from constituting the dominant force in the social formation as a whole. The full powers of the state, above all its ability to mobilize the latent energies of the unconscious in support of its parental persona, remain largely in the background, save for periods of overt internal disruption or external war, so that the forces of capital exert the preponderant active influence in normal times. During these periods, the state advances the interests of capital as a natural response to the appeals of capital, as well as in a calculating fashion to promote its own peacetime strength. Thus the general ideologies and basic interests of capital usually exert their sway without opposition, giving coherence to the social formation of capitalism as a regime of capital, first and foremost. But that is not the same thing as claiming that these interests always prevail in what Engels called the "last instance." In the schism of realms, it is enough to establish the primacy of capital, not its dictatorship.

## V

We turn now to an aspect of the political nature of capitalism to which we have not yet paid attention. This

---

10. See Albert Bergeson, ed., *Studies of the Modern World-System* (New York: Academic Press, 1980), esp. Ch. 10.

is an unnoticed masking of functions that have been bifurcated between two realms, so that the business world quite unwittingly carries out a primary task of government, and the state tacitly discharges a central task of economic provisioning.

What is the basic function of government? Its activities are as diverse as the provision of laws and sanctions, the conduct of military affairs, the celebration of secular and religious occasions; the building of public works and monuments; the gathering of information; the establishment of social well-being. In and of themselves, these tasks are technical and organizational. What makes them "political" is that they are carried out on behalf of ruling personages or classes. The military adventures, the laws and sanctions, the celebrations and monuments—even the administration of welfare—reflect the aims and purposes of the dominant class about whose character I will speak in the next chapter. As such, the state's political function is partly defensive and partly promotive, depending on whether it is justifying or enforcing the *raisons d'être* of this class or advancing its interests through projects that mobilize and inspire the energies and imagination of the populace. Thus the political function is by no means the exclusive prerogative of the state. Indeed, all activities, including the normal operations of the army, the church, the educational apparatus, and of course the activities of production and distribution, take on a political aspect insofar as they legitimate the existing structure of privilege, or express the interest of the ruling element.

Like the tasks of government, the direct activities of the economic realm are also technical and organizational. The core economic function consists in the provision of the requisite flows of goods and labor power needed to sustain a desired stream of output. From this point of view, economics is a form of "social engineering," as distant from political considerations as the specifications of materials needed to sustain a given load for a bridge.

The political aspect of economic activity enters because the engineer is in the service of some dominant group, capitalist, imperial, or whatever. As such, the engineer who supervises the "functional" organization of production is guided by the prevailing interest-system, which not only designates the ends for which he must plan his means but which also establishes the calculus—and beneath the calculus, the concepts—by which the rationality of the means themselves are established. We have already seen that capitalism imposes such a calculus in the form of profit considerations, and *mutatis mutandis,* so it is with the economic calculations that express the interests of slave economies, serfdoms, aristocracies, and the like.

This general discussion is enough to indicate that of necessity the political and economic realms interpenetrate in all societies—or more accurately, that considerations of an "economizing" kind, although with differing criteria, are to be found in all activities of rulership, and that decisions of a political kind, although with differing interests at stake, are inherent in all systems of material production. This is not yet, however, the masking of functions that becomes a distinctive attribute of capitalism and an important element in shaping its nature. The masking refers to the fact that under capitalism, where a realm of economic affairs has been separated from the matrix of the body politic, the distribution of "economic" and "political" functions takes place in a manner that, like in so many instances in capitalism, conceals and disguises the actual processes at work.

Here it is useful to begin by reflecting again on the matter of coercion, the indispensable means by which the surplus is obtained under tributary systems. In the capitalist era, as we know, the coercive rights of the ruling class disappear, to be replaced by the generalized pressure of market forces bearing down on a work force that has been separated from the means of production, which are owned as private capital. As we have already discussed, this means that power can no longer be exerted from master to man, or from lord to serf. All that remains is the "free" market relation between capital-owning and capital-needing classes. Yet, despite the disappearance of coercion and exaction, surplus continues to be generated by the system and to flow upward from the producing to the dominant levels, whether composed of merchants, corporate capitalists, state officials, or combinations of these. Thus, in a manner that we have already examined, the unconstrained interplay of the activities of workers and capitalists produces an upward-flowing stream of profits that yields the same political benefits to the dominant class as under tributary regimes, although the proportions between top and bottom incomes are likely to be much less lopsided under capitalism.

Still more significant, because still more concealed, is a second manner in which political power is exercised within the economic realm. This is the delegation of the power to command labor—quite literally to direct its disposition, as did the Pharaohs when they gathered their gangs for the construction of the pyramids. Under capitalism, the direct allocation of labor is virtually surrendered by the state, with the exception of its military forces. Instead, the tasks of labor discipline and command are placed in the hands of employers, who carry on this essentially political task with virtually no awareness that in doing so they are not only furthering their private interests but discharging a function that, stripped of its market aspects, would be instantly recognizable as that of the commanders of labor gangs, peasants, or slaves.

As we already know, the function carried on in this condition of total unawareness is that of exploiting a labor force—a political act that is unmistakable when a lord wrests his share from a serf's crops but that becomes invisible when the same diversion of output is carried out by the market mechanism. To make this statement is by no means to deny that the worker's lot is immeasurably freer under the dispensation of the market than under that of the direct coercive oversight. The conservative defenders of capitalism do not misstate the case when they emphasize the difference between free and forced labor. It is, however, precisely because the worker under capitalism is free to quit and to appeal at law if the wage contract has been abrogated that the continuing exploitative diversion of surplus remains unnoticed.

So, too, does the continuation of another aspect of the political function—the disciplining of labor—so readily observable in nonwage relationships. This disciplinary function, as political in its way as the extraction of surplus, includes the right of capital—although not without limitations—to determine the physical requirements of the task, the tools and equipment with which it is conducted, the pace of work, the purpose and geographical locations of the endeavor, and the right to discontinue employment. It is these aspects, more than the wage that is "set" by market forces, where the political authority formerly vested in bailiffs and overseers appears as the prerogative of the capitalist. As R. H. Tawney has written:

> . . . [T]he man who employs, governs, to the extent of the number of men employed. He has jurisdiction over them. He occupies what is really a public office. He has power, not of pit and gallows . . . but of overtime and short time, full bellies and empty bellies, health and sickness. . . . [11]

Tawney emphasizes this governing power in terms of the capacity of employers to affect the well-being of their employees. What even he does not see is that the exercise of the very right to organize production itself—to choose both its means and its ends—is an exercise of political power, an instance of domination. The deployment of the legal authority of the capitalist within the confines of his business enterprise thus constitutes an unrecognized transfer of political power from the state into private hands. As Ellen Meiksins Wood has put it, capitalism represents "the ultimate 'privatization' of politics, to the extent that functions formerly associated with coercive political power . . . are now firmly lodged in the private sphere. . . . "[12]

---

11. Taken from "R. H. Tawney's Commonplace Book," *Dissent,* Fall 1981, p. 490.

12. Ellen Meiksins Wood, "The Separation of the Economic and the Politi-

The other side of the coin—the incorporation of economic functions within the political arm of the capitalist state—takes several forms. There is the immediate use of state power for the protection of activities within the economic realm, above all in the provision of the law and order essential for the preservation of the system of material provisioning and surplus generation. As all theorists from Hobbes and Locke and Smith agree, a primary duty of the government is to insure the rights of property: "The acquisition of valuable and extensive property," writes Smith in *The Wealth of Nations,* "necessarily requires the establishment of civil government.[13]

Less fully understood is the function of the state in undertaking the tasks needed to sustain the economic realm. This function is described by Smith and others as the duty of "erecting and maintaining those public institutions and those public works which . . . may be in the highest degree advantageous to a great society . . . [but] could never repay the expense to any individual or small number of individuals. . . . "[14]

What seems to be only a "public" duty of government has, however, another masked aspect. It is the manner in which inputs needed for the accumulation of capital, but unprofitable to produce within the market framework, can be provided to the economic realm. From this viewpoint

---

13. Smith, *Wealth of Nations,* p. 710. In his (transcribed) *Lectures on Jurisprudence* (1762–63), Smith is quoted as being even more out-spoken: "Laws and government may be considered in this and indeed in every case as a combination of the rich to oppress the poor, and preserve to themselves the inequality of goods which would otherwise soon be destroyed by the attacks of the poor, who if not hindered by government would soon reduce the others to an equality with themselves by open violence" (Oxford: Clarendon Press, 1978, p. 208).

14. Smith, *Wealth of Nations,* p. 681.

the state does not merely add "public" works to private ones. Rather, it accepts from the economic realm whatever necessary undertakings cannot remain in it. In these cases, the state foists upon the public the costs of those activities that would result in monetary "losses" if they were carried out by the economic sphere, while recognizing as inviolable the right of private enterprise to benefit from its profitable undertakings. This socialization of losses applies to much of the network of canals, railways, highways, and airways that have played an indispensable part in capitalist growth, as well as the provision of literate and socialized work forces through public education programs, the protection of public health, and the like. All these are examples of "public works," behind whose manifest usefulness for the citizenry at large lies the latent *economic* function of providing necessary inputs for the operations of the M-C-M' circuit, and the *political* function of strengthening the regime of the dominant class.

I do not wish to lose my point by overstatement, as if a genuine public interest were not also a part of democratic capitalist policies. But in the great majority of programs, what appear to be purely neutral or benevolent functions of the state become, on close scrutiny, assumptions of necessary undertakings whose drain on private surplus would be too great to bear and which are therefore borne by the public realm—transportation networks as the classic case. Such an assumption of necessary support is not limited to capitalism by any means—the Romans had their dole, their circuses, their public works—but the openly avowed purpose of these interventions was to maintain the existing imperial framework. Under the masking of functions characteristic of a capitalist system this open declaration of purpose gives way to the elaborate pretense of a private realm operating without any—or with only a minimal—support from the state, and of a state only marginally responsible for the successful operation of the economic sphere.

Last, there is the direct use of state power, diplomatic and military, to encourage or protect economic activity. Here we have only to recall the use of naval power in the seventeenth and eighteenth centuries by the Dutch, French, English, and American governments to secure and protect their commercial markets; the waging of wars in the nineteenth and twentieth centuries for mineral and other rights to be exploited by the economic sector; and the general sensitivity of the governing arm of society to threats, foreign or domestic, against its economic "way of life."

Thus there are vital economic functions exercised by the governing branch of capitalism just as there are powerful political ones exercised by its economic branch. It is here, indeed, that the political key to the system lies, not merely in the creation of a world of business, with its realm of contractual freedom distinct from that of politics, but in the mystifying diffusion of political and economic powers and functions within both worlds. From this ill-understood and camouflaged partitioning of the unitary powers of the precapitalist state stems a great deal of the general misperception that surrounds the nature of capitalism with its presumed public and private "sectors," a confusion shared by the members of its governing and business echelons, as well as by the public at large.[15]

*It is therefore a profound mistake to conceive of capitalism as being in essence a "private" economic system.* It is unquestionably an historic mark of identification of capitalism that it relies on the activities of formally uncoordinated units of production and distribution both to assure its continuance and to give rise to its surplus. It is here, without doubt, that the source of its dynamic energies and technological inventiveness must be sought. At the same time, it must be evident that not all the necessary inputs for such a society can be provided by the economic realm. Passing over such conventional exceptions as the means of external and internal military force, the normal operation of the market system would be unsustainable without the socializing, protecting, and stimulating state activities that further the regime of capital. These services are of sufficient importance for the working of the system so that they are provided at or below cost to assure their general availability: were they not so important, many of them could be provided by business at a high enough price. Thus the division between state and economy is not one of extrinsic function—the political realm concerned with "public" needs, the economic realm with "private" ones.

---

15. In *Multinational Companies and Nation States* (1975) Robin Murray provides a useful categorization of some of these *res publica,* which I condense as follows: 1) the guaranteeing of property rights, backed by force; 2) economic liberalization in the abolition of restrictions on the movement of economic agents or commodities within the national territory; 3) economic orchestration, such as planning or mitigation of crises; 4) provision of infrastructure, such as a trained labor supply; 5) intervention for social consensus in mitigating disruptive effects of accumulation; and 6) the managment of external relations, including war, trade, financial arrangements, etc. I have sketched in some of these major activities in Chapter 6. Reference from A. G. Frank, *Crisis: In The Third World* (New York: Holmes & Meiers, 1980), pp. 231–32.

The essential difference is rather one of the possibility of the recapture of expenditure in the marketplace. What the economic realm can do, the government is generally enjoined from doing. That which business cannot do, but which requires to be done, becomes the business of the public sector.

It is equally evident that the designation of capitalism as "self-ordering," while unmistakably the case in comparison to tributary systems, must also be understood in a qualified sense. The term implies that all *essential* activities connected with the material process can be, at least in principle, consigned to the market. We have seen that this is untrue, not alone in the case of such goods as defense, for which no marketing system seems imaginable, but in the broad historical reality of capitalism as a self-reproducing social formation. Here the state, both as defender and promoter of the economic realm, has played so prominent a role that even the most abstract scenarios of the system unwittingly assign it a central and indispensable place when they take as their unit of conceptual analysis *the state*. Remove the regime of capital and the state would remain, although it might change dramatically; remove the state and the regime of capital would not last a day. In this sense politics is prior to economics in that domination must precede exploitation. Thus once again we encounter the tense relation of realms characteristic of the social formation in which capital calls the tune by which the state normally dances but takes for granted that the state will provide the theater within which the performance takes place.

All this mocks the conventional economic view that the

public realm is somehow secondary or ancillary to the private realm, and that a market system can be adequately represented and even studied in models that omit the loss-absorbing, momentum-imparting political domain, with its curiously concealed economic functions. But it is precisely this concealment—the consequence of the fissioning of unitary empires into state and economy—that is another instance of the capacity of capitalism to enthrall and becloud the understanding of its members, in many respects the most powerful of the ways in which the nature of the system affects behavior and belief.

# 5

# The Ideology of Capital

THE ISSUE OF BELIEF takes us to ideology—
the deeply and unselfconsciously held views
of the dominant class in any social order. Here it is important to begin by distinguishing these beliefs from views
held in a more pietistic or even cynical fashion, to manipu-
late or form the opinions of those who are not members
of the ruling class. Unlike such propaganda, ideologies are
systems of thought and belief by which dominant classes
explain *to themselves* how their social system operates and
what principles it exemplifies. Ideological systems therefore exist not as fictions but as "truths"—and not only
evidential truths but moral truths.[1]

Capitalist ideology has exactly the same explanatory
function as does that of feudal or tributary systems of
belief. But as with other aspects of capitalism, it differs in
decisive ways from earlier belief systems. Samir Amin has
pointed out that the ideologies of earlier social formations
were typically "world" religions—Hinduism, Confucianism, Islam, the divine rulerships of early Mesoamerican

---

1. See Goran Therborn, *What Does the Ruling Class Do When It Rules?*
(London: Verso, 1978), pp. 171–73; also Joyce Oldham Appleby, *Economic
Thought and Ideology in Seventeenth-Century England* (Princeton, N.J.: Prince-
ton University Press, 1978), pp. 5–6.

and Near Eastern kingdoms, Christianity. As such, these ideologies further expressed the essential unity of tributary societies. The full authority of a priesthood sanctioned the exercise of worldly rule, including its use for the collection of surplus; and this surplus was used, in turn, to support religious institutions. A single legitimating view, sacred in origin, thereby fortified the existing regime. Even when disputes broke out between priestly orders and secular authorities, the struggles continued the tradition of state religion, with one monolithic conception striving to oust another—Buddhism competing against Hinduism, Taoism against Confucianism, Protestantism against the Catholic church.[2]

The ideological aspect of capitalism differs fundamentally from this imperial form. It is not sacred but secular, not monolithic but many-faceted. Its emplacement therefore requires more than a palace coup in which one absolute belief displaces another. The installation of the ideology of capitalism rather resembles a popular revolution, not only calling on new forms of social explanation but seeking a new source—in actuality, new sources—of legitimacy powerful enough to challenge the authority of a universal church.

## II

Historically, the development of bourgeois self-clarification proceeded along several fronts. One of these was

---

2. Amin, *Class and Nation,* p. 52. There was no world religion as such for the social formation of feudalism. Rather, the tenets of Christianity and those of secular vassalage combined to form a framework of divided authority—the "two swords"—within a system of shared values. See Georges Duby, *The Three Orders* (Chicago: University of Chicago Press, 1982).

the forging of a new attitude toward the central activity of the capitalist socioeconomic system—the search for profit. In every pre-capitalist society we find acquisitive activity disliked or despised—in part as a projection of aristocratic attitudes (true aristocrats do not "need" money); in part as an expression of popular revulsion against money lenders and exploitative local traders; in part perhaps as a deep-rooted protest against the de-personalization of monetary dealings. Nowhere was this distaste more pronounced than within Christianity, where the taking of ordinary interest was declared to be an ex-communicable offense as late as the Council of Vienne in 1311, and where three centuries later a disapproving view of wealth-seeking continued to inform Protestant as well as Catholic religious sentiments, even after both churches had made their formal truce with profits and interest.

This low estimation of acquisitiveness does not disap-pear with the rise in the power and influence of the bour-geois class. "In the numerous treatises on the passions that appeared in the seventeenth century," writes Albert Hirschman in *The Passions and the Interests,* "no change whatever can be found in the assessment of avarice as 'the foulest of them all' or in its position as the deadliest Deadly Sin that it had come to occupy toward the end of the Middle Ages."[3] Even in the worldly eighteenth cen-tury, it is very much in the spirit of the age that Adam Smith regards acquisitiveness, in both the *Theory of Moral Sentiments* and *The Wealth of Nations,* as a useful but

---

3. Albert Hirschman, *The Passions and the Interests* (Princeton, N.J.: Princeton University Press, 1977), p. 41.

never admirable characteristic, leading to the pursuit of things that, viewed with philosophic detachment, appear "contemptible and trifling," or simply "vulgar."[4]

That which did change, making it possible by the seventeenth or eighteenth century to create an acceptable belief system around activities that only a few centuries earlier would have been regarded as anathema and that continued to be denigrated, was the appraisal of the consequences of acquisitive behavior. Here we see two separate movements. One of them, analyzed by Hirschman, involved the reinterpretation of avarice or love of lucre, not as a disruptive "passion" but as a steadying "interest." As such, the drive for wealth was perceived as a calming influence compared with the unruly disposition over which no similar rational, calculating attribute exerted its restraints. In the guise of commerce, acquisitiveness is thus seen to exert a civilizing effect—*le doux commerce*—a point of view we find expressed again in Adam Smith, who writes that "probity and punctuality" are virtues that invariably accompany the introduction of commercial relations into society.[5]

The second movement toward the rationalization of acquisitive behavior lies in the development of a "science" of acquisition. This is, of course, the discipline of political economy, later economics, that emerges in the seventeenth, and achieves its full-fledged expression in the eighteenth, century. The very possibility of such a science itself

---

4. Adam Smith, *Theory of Moral Sentiments*, p. 183; *Wealth of Nations*, p. 342.

5. Hirschman, *Passions and Interests*, p. 41; Smith, *Lectures on Jurisprudence*, p. 538. ("*Doux commerce*" is to be translated as "gentle," not "sweet," commerce.)

implies that acquisitive behavior has lost its connection with the unruly passions and has come to be regarded as a steady principle of human "motion," capable of measurement and restraint. The ideological aspect of the new science emerges, however, when we inquire into the purpose of political economy or economics. As we have already had ample occasion to see, it is an explanation of how the commercial or nascent industrial system works, *from the point of view of the ruling class.* This does not imply a willful distortion of the collective effects of acquisitiveness but rather a presentation that takes into its purview certain aspects of the process, while excluding others.

We have already looked into one crucial aspect of this ideological view of the economic process in our discussion of the fetishism of commodities—the extraordinary spell cast by the commodity form of labor (and its precondition, capital). It is this fetishism that still causes economists to perceive the process of production as carried on by M. le Capital and Mme. la Terre (in Marx's words), as well as by the "factor of production" called labor. It is largely as a consequence of this unconscious attitude that modern-day economics has no concept of any "surplus" that is systematically transferred into the hands of a dominant class. It is worth repeating that economics explains the flows of interest and dividends and rent, of trading gains, industrial profits, or technological advantage as the "earnings" of capital. It thereby confuses the incomes that accrue to the owners of capital *because they have agreed not to withhold their property from use* with the actual physical contribution these resources create when placed in use. It follows that economics has no explanation for the origin of profits other than the "imperfections" (such as monopoly or transient technological rents) that separate the real world from the state of general static equilibrium that is presumed to represent the logic of the system. Thus the very category of economic life that more than any other distinguishes the regime of capital from all others disappears from sight.

Rather than belabor this aspect of economics as ideology, I wish to call attention to a less commonly remarked aspect of the "science," exemplified in Locke's *Second Treatise on Government,* whose explication of the wage labor relation we have noted earlier. In his famous Chapter V, "Of Property," Locke sets out to demonstrate that *unlimited* private acquisition, for centuries the target of the most scathing religious and philosophic criticism, was in fact compatible with both the dictates of Scripture and the promptings of right reason.

The objections to unlimited acquisition, Locke points out, are two: that acquisitiveness may impoverish others, and that it may waste goods that could be used by others. Thus the injunctions imposed on acquisition by Scripture and reason are that "enough and as good" must be left behind for all, and that "Nothing was made by God for man to spoil or destroy." These injunctions would seem to constrain the scale of private accumulation to that of petty proprietorships. But Locke shows that no such inhibitions need in fact obtain. For an accumulator who encloses land and cultivates it *increases its yield,* so that the act of acquiring land creates more wealth, which is presumably available to others. And the possibility of holding one's wealth in the form of gold, which neither spoils nor goes to waste, evades the spoilage that would prohibit the accumulation of perishable commodities.

Thus Locke disposes of a question that had almost monopolized the attention of social critics of the past, namely the moral significance of acquisition. By dwelling on the capacity of acquisitiveness to increase the amount of wealth, Locke changes the generation of surplus from a zero sum game, where every gain is someone's loss, into a positive sum process in which every person's enrichment is at least potentially the occasion for the enrichment of all. The ideological—as contrasted with the analytic—contribution of this argument does not lie in the empirical validity of Locke's claim which passes too easily over the question of how widely the gains from accumulation will be shared). The ideological breakthrough concerns a reinterpretation of an aspect of the acquisitive process that had formerly exerted a steady negative influence, often ignored in fact but never forgotten in principle. This was the morally destructive impact of the accumulation of wealth *on the gatherer himself.* The legend of Midas speaks volumes here, for Midas's curse has nothing to do with any impoverishment that his passion for gold would impose on others. It was to this ancient threat of self-destruction that Locke applies the remedy of an assurance that the accumulation of wealth violated neither the canons of right reason nor the Scriptures, so that the question of moral unease could in good conscience be set to one side.

Adam Smith's position on this issue is interesting because Smith was by no means oblivious to the moral costs of acquisitiveness. In his Glasgow lectures, delivered more than ten years before the publication of *The Wealth of Nations,* he balanced his praise of commerce for bringing probity and punctuality by pointing out that it also "sinks the courage of mankind, and tends to extinguish martial spirit. . . . By having their minds constantly employed on the arts of luxury [the people] grow effeminate and dastardly."[6] Later, in the *Wealth,* Smith often lashes out at the motives of merchants and deplores the ignorance and apathy into which the working classes fall as a direct consequence of their exposure to the accumulation process, with its use of the mechanical division of labor. Yet despite these strictures, as outspoken as any that Marx was to offer, Smith's estimation of the positive effects of accumulation clearly outweighs his assessment of their costs. For all its balance, the *Wealth* is a book dedicated to the legitimation of an acquisitive, capital-amassing society, and that final balance could not be struck if the moral costs of such a society were not, in Smith's mind, overbalanced by its material benefits.

In Smith's hands the interplay of material progress and moral decline takes the form of a subtle dialectic that invests his work with its remarkable depths. In the hands of his successors the dialectic disappears, and the evaluation of economic growth emphasizes its material aspects without any concern as to untoward moral consequences, in terms of either motives or social outcomes. This deemphasis on the moral aspect of economic life takes a final and decisive turn in the early nineteenth century with the

---

6. Smith, *Lectures,* p. 540.

advent of Bentham's utilitarian philosophy. Now any last lingering doubts about greed and rapacity, as well as exploitation and luxury, are removed by the demonstration that the happiness of all can be achieved—in fact, can *only* be achieved—by the self-regarding pursuit of the happiness of each. If the accumulation of wealth yields happiness for the individual, it follows that it will provide it for the society.

This is not the place to analyze the premises of utilitarianism, except to mention that it achieved its brilliant analytic results by ruling out of bounds the very question to be answered: namely, whether ancient canons of "virtue" and "justice"—canons that were always founded on a scrutiny of motives and an "external" assessment of social results—could in fact be replaced by a system that declared these canons to be arbitrary, and therefore null and void.[7] What is significant for our purposes is that the utilitarian framework provided the final resolution of the moral dilemmas of the economic process by its assertion that whatever served the individual served society. By logical analogy, whatever created a profit (and thereby served the individual capitalist) also served society, so that a blanket moral exemption was, so to speak, extended over the entire range of activity that passed the profit-and-loss test of the marketplace.*

---

7. See Alisdair MacIntyre, *After Virtue* (Notre Dame, Indiana: University of Notre Dame Press, 1981).

*I cannot resist adding an example of the modern use of economics as a system of clarificatory belief. Thomas Schelling writes: " . . . [T]he free market may not do much, or anything, to distribute opportunities and resources among people the way you and I might like them distributed . . . ; it may encourage individualistic rather than group values. It may lead to assymetrical personal

The consequences of this ideological clarification were, and continue to be, far greater than is commonly understood. The de-moralization of economic activity not only removed any need to justify the logic of capitalism, provided that it did not directly violate the law or outrage the deepest moral standards of society, but it made meaningless such questions as: Which of two equally profitable undertakings is the better? Can one call wasteful any undertaking that returns a satisfactory profit? Is it possible to condemn on moral grounds legal and profitable actions, such as the decision to relocate a plant at the cost of community disruption? Thus a kind of moral pardon is applied to all licit activities of the capital-accumulating sector, although in the so-called public sector, where the absorption of losses rather than the accumulation of capital takes place, no such justification is available, so that moral obloquy and standards are constantly brought to bear.

As a result there is a further widening of the schism of realms: one "private," profitable, and above intrinsic reproach; the other public, unprofitable, and without the presumptive innocence of the private sector. The ideology of economics plays an indispensable part in holding apart

---

relationships between employee and employer. . . . The market may even perform disastrously when inflation and depression are concerned. Still, within these serious limitations, it does remarkably well in coordinating or harmonizing or integrating the effects of . . . individuals and organizations" (*Micromotives and Macrobehavior* [New York: W.W. Norton, 1978]), p. 23. Schelling is by no means a bland "apologist" for the market system. Note, however, that the market is given its ultimate blessing on terms that excuse a maldistribution of opportunities and resources, unsocial values, unequal bargaining power, and perhaps "disastrous" performance during inflation or depression. One is tempted to ask by what criteria the system would be deemed a failure.

activities that, from our perspective, can be seen to inter-mingle, and in determining what criteria are regarded as appropriate for the assessment of each.

Here I must add once again that the purpose of an ideology is not to mystify but to clarify; not to mislead the lower classes but to enlighten all classes, in particular, the ruling class. Economics does not "legitimate" activities that in fact the ruling class knows in its heart of hearts to be wrong. It succeeds, rather, in offering definitions of right and wrong that exonerate the activities and results of market activity. This is accomplished in part because the motives of acquisitiveness are reclassified as interests and not passions; in part because the benefits of material gain are judged to outweigh any deterioration in the moral quality of society; and last and most important because the term "goodness" is equated with *private* happiness, ab-solving all licit activity from any need to justify itself on other grounds. These powerful prescriptions, ground into the lenses through which the ruling class observes its own actions, provide the moral self-assurance without which it could not carry on its historic mission with such dedicated conviction.

A second, equally fraught consequence of the ideology of economics concerns the widely recognized phenome-non of the "commercialization" of life. From one capital-ist nation to the next, the thresholds and boundaries over which economic activity is allowed to step may vary, but looking backward for a generation or two, it is clear that in all capitalist nations more and more of "private," that is, self-determined, life in fact becomes public life, insofar as it is determined by the regime of capital. Thus to take two familiar instances, athletic prowess, one of the oldest and proudest activities of private individuals, has everywhere become a matter of commercial "sport," and the self-determination of life patterns, the most private of all activities, is everywhere deliberately subjected to the influence of "advertising," the purpose of which is to induce individuals, without knowing anything of them, to change their mode of living. These instances of a relentless commercialization, perhaps the single most self-destructive process of modern capitalist civilization, could be multiplied manifold.

What is needed is to understand the process as part of the nature of the system. Commercialization is a consequence of commodification—the continuous search of business for areas of social activity that can be subsumed within the capital-generating circuit. We are familiar with this process from our previous examination of the roots of capital's self-expansion. To this understanding we can now add a dimension of ideology. The expansion of capital is aided and abetted by the declaration that moral and aesthetic criteria—the only dikes that might hold back the floodtide of capital's expansion—are *without relevance* within the realm of economic activity. To turn the coin over, we might say that the images of consumption projected by advertising are a kind of "capitalist realism," the analogue to the pictures of collectivized contentment featured in the poster art of "socialist realism."[8] This is the crucial element of understanding that ideology brings to capitalism.

---

8. See Michael Schudson, *Advertising: The Uneasy Persuasion* (New York: Basic Books, 1984), Ch. 7.

## III

We have already had ample occasion to note that the relation between business and state becomes a central political problem for capitalism as the consequence of the appearance of two distinct realms within the regime of capital. It is not surprising, then, that the explanation of the proper relation of these two realms becomes a central question, even an obsession, for political thought under capitalism.

The indispensable requirement for the effective exercise of political authority is legitimacy. In tributary systems this issue arises when claimants to the imperium contend, but the intrinsic nature of rule itself is never a point at issue. This is because rulership is viewed as the secular aspect of the religious essence of such societies. Rulers derive their authority from the godhead; and whereas the genealogy or conduct of a particular ruler may be questionable, the inherent legitimacy of government itself—of the right to rulership to exist—is beyond question.

Bourgeois thought represents the polar opposite of this imperial presupposition. Government is no longer considered to be a natural, timeless attribute of all social collectivities but is seen as the creation of "individuals" who band together for their mutual safety and protection. Nothing symbolizes this more vividly than the original frontispiece of Hobbes's *Leviathan*—itself a charter document in the formulation of such a social covenant—with its great figure of a sovereign looming like a giant over the horizon, a sovereign whose armor, on close inspection, reveals itself to be composed of the tiny figures of a multitude of individuals.

Such a view of government is founded on a wholly new view of the relation between the social whole and its constituent members. Whereas in all previous systems one individual alone is considered to be no more than the dust of a shattered social organism, in bourgeois societies he or she is imagined to be a self-sufficient cell from which a living social organism is constructed. That which is ideological about this political conception is not just its fictive history but the assumptions about the nature of the "individuals" who meet to form governments. These are not persons perceived as individuated members of an existing, aboriginal social organization. They are imagined as isolated personages existing without any social ties—self-supporting yet mutually dependent hermits, coexisting in a state of latent hostility and suspicion: Hobbes's "time of Warre, where every man is Enemy to every man." Familial contacts aside, they interact at arm's length, through market exchanges and contractual obligations.

The concept of this monadic individual is foundational for many aspects of bourgeois ideology. It rapidly becomes the premise of its economics. As we have seen, it is a necessary assumption for a utilitarian approach to social welfare, where the outcome is entirely dependent on the requirement that individuals consult only *their own* states of contentment and act accordingly. Most important of all, it becomes the basis for the "liberal" view of government.

There are many definitions of classical political liberalism, but all agree that its central conception is a constriction of political authority, to create the largest possible space for the self-determined action of "individuals." Political liberalism accordingly envisages a main function of government as a self-inhibitory discipline, withdrawing from areas previously occupied by state authority and creating legal barriers to secure those liberated territories for their inhabitants' unfettered use.

The particular kind of use uppermost in the minds of the intellectual fathers of liberalism was the economic act of participating in the market bargain—the main binding act of a society in which the order-bestowing functions of government have been curtailed. Although the individual worker's need to be freed from all forms of legally enforceable subservience was always a central tenet of liberalism, the prototypical economic actor for whose purposes this liberal design was intended was the merchant or nascent industrial capitalist, for his social effectiveness required the right to conduct his affairs as he wished and to be quit of government-enforced obligations beyond those explicitly included within his contractual agreements.

Thus the ideological element in political liberalism, like that in economics, resides not so much in any apologetics —although those were often enough found in the arguments built on their premises—but in the explication of the appropriate functions of the two realms for the enlightenment of the ruling class itself. Economics, as we know, explains the positive effects of a generalized search for capital and "explains away" any inhibitory reservations with respect to the moral consequences of unleashing the acquisitive drive through society. Political liberalism explains the appropriate activities of the governing branch as the partner of a society that has already accepted and legitimated individual accumulation. As Locke puts it, echoing the sentiments of Hobbes and anticipating those of Smith, "The great and chief end . . . of men's uniting into commonwealths and putting themselves under government is the preservation of their property."[9]

In no way does this negate, or even denigrate, the broader concern of political liberalism with freedom and with the protection of personal, political, and intellectual rights against government intervention. The initial struggles of liberalism, such as the Glorious Revolution of 1688, antedate the advent of capitalism and involve political and social more than economic rights. But with the solidification of these rights, the issue of *economic* freedom comes to the fore among other freedoms, and with the assured protection of private property, the issue of economic *freedom* comes to the fore among the prerogatives of property.

Given the bifurcation of functions between the economic and political spheres characteristic of the new order, it is not surprising that the central issue then becomes the relation of "government" to the freedoms of the economic realm. The resolution of this issue takes the form of the policy of laissez faire, the distinctive economic stance of political liberalism. Laissez faire was never intended to signify that there was to be no "interference" by government within the economic realm. Adam Smith, whose delineation of government power was extremely

---

9. John Locke, *The Second Treatise of Government,* p. 71. Locke's concept of property extends beyond chattels into a view of personhood, but it is nonetheless unimaginable without chattels or personal wealth.

pragmatic, gave his blessing to the provision of national defense, the establishment of justice, and the provision of necessary public works—allocations of authority sufficient to establish a very considerable and influential government presence. Fifty years after Smith, John Stuart Mill defended laissez faire as "the general rule," "every departure from [which] unless required by some great good, is a certain evil." Nonetheless, he declared, "in the particular circumstances of a given age or nation, there is scarcely anything really important to the general interest, which it may not be desirable, or even necessary, that the government should take upon itself."[10]

That which endows this perception of government with its ideological character lies in the manner in which the issue is conceived, not that in which it is resolved. Like the unwitting depiction of the individual as possessing the attributes and requirements of an active participant in a market system, the conception of laissez faire, and of the political liberalism of which it is an expression, is that "the economy" is a realm not unlike that of "the government," save that it possesses no territory of its own. *The ideological problem for capitalism thus arises from the need to explicate rulership in a society where two structures of authority occupy the same space, engage the activities and command the obedience of the same persons, but fail to recognize their complementary coexistence.*

The outcome is that government treats with the economy, and to some extent the economy treats with government, much as do two foreign nations. Emissaries are

---

10. Mill, *Principles of Political Economy,* pp. 944–45, 970.

exchanged as personnel move from one sphere to the other; treaties are negotiated as laws; spheres of influence are defined and recognized as policy. This process of accommodation is rendered difficult by virtue of the frequently conflicting relations between the two spheres—business mainly desiring encouragement and protection in its task of seeking surplus; government charged with the necessity to reconcile, adjudicate, and on occasion to restrain or redirect this process through its law-making power. This inherently difficult problem is made more complex as internal and external developments alter the relative importance of the two branches; and the entire process is rendered still more complicated by virtue of the misperceived nature of the division of functions that exists under capitalism.

Last and by no means least is the tension that arises because of the differently construed boundaries of each realm, that of capital limited by the extent of the market, that of the political sphere by formal territorial demarcations. Each of these boundaries is, in fact, ambiguous. Capital exerts its magnetic influence across national boundaries as effectively as within them but lacks the protective presence of "its own" political sphere when it operates abroad. Thus, as we have seen in our last chapter, the regime of capital has an intrinsic dependency on the enforcement power that resides in the political sphere, just as the state has an intrinsic dependency on the fortunes of the regime of capital, including its international activities, as the precondition for its own political success. The ambiguity of boundaries and the mutual dependencies of realms have gained special prominence in our own day but can be discerned far back in earlier stages of capitalism,

with its long history of indecisive capital-government relationships in mercantile policy, tariff and trade regulation,
and in the often strained exercise of military and economic
imperialism.

I must not neglect, although I do not intend to dwell on,
one last aspect of the ideology of political power—the
relationship of liberalism, with its central preoccupation
with the separation of political from economic life, and
democracy in the broad sense of political freedom. I shall
be brief; not from any failure to recognize the importance
of the problem, but because I wish to consider the manner
in which this burning question is *understood*—that is, its
ideological aspect—rather than the manner in which it is
answered in history.

The difference between the two is very great. The historical relationship between capitalism and democracy is
complex. Milton Friedman, a staunch advocate of the
view that political freedom can only be attained within a
framework of capitalist relations, is forthright in acknowl-
edging that capitalism is not in itself a guarantor of freedom. "It is clearly possible to have economic arrangements that are fundamentally capitalist and political
arrangements that are not free," he writes, citing the instances of Tsarist Russia, Fascist Spain and Italy, Japan
between the two World Wars, and Nazi Germany, to
which we could add the cases of the United States, until
the mid-twentieth century, and of the Union of South
Africa up to this moment, with respect to their black
populations.[11]

---

11. Milton Friedman, *Capitalism and Freedom* (Chicago: University of
Chicago Press, 1962), p. 10.

Given this uncertainty, it is not surprising that there exists no overarching explanation of the circumstances in which political freedom is preserved or destroyed within a capitalist setting. Rather, from one case to the next we explain the course of events by referring to the effects of differing political institutions, national traditions, cultural patterns, charismatic leaders, military or economic reverses, and so on. That is only to admit that we possess no general theory as to why democracy triumphs in one capitalist nation and fails in another.

There is nevertheless one striking generalization that can be extracted from the otherwise indeterminate history of democracy. It is that political freedom in modern times —we leave aside the "democracy" of ancient Greece or the participatory life of primitive societies—has only appeared in capitalist states. To put the generalization in its more powerful negative form, democratic liberties have not yet appeared, except fleetingly, in any nation that has declared itself to be fundamentally anticapitalist, which is to say within the self-styled "Marxist" socialist ambit. The tendency in all these nations has been toward restrictive, usually repressive governments that have systematically compressed or extinguished political and civil liberties. Thus despite our inability to generalize about the conditions for the success of democracy within capitalism, there is powerful evidence in modern history to suggest some "logic" for its failure to succeed in anticapitalist milieus.

Here the central argument of political liberalism is that the separation of realms creates the essential conditions for political freedom because the state cannot enforce its will through economic sanctions, such as denying work to political dissidents. The argument gains its cogency because it is grounded in the structural division of realms that is an intrinsic aspect of the regime of capital. Private property may be an inherently exploitative institution, but it is also potentially a protective one.* Other means of enforcing subservience exist than that of crude economic force—Anthony Giddens stresses the surveillance capabilities of the modern state—but it seems fair to suggest that some kind of relatively inviolable nonstate employment sector is a condition for political freedom as we know it.[12]

For all its persuasiveness, it is still necessary to subject this central contention of political liberalism to scrutiny for its ideological elements—that is, for the preconceptions of a regime of capital that are unknowingly insinuated into the terms of the argument. Here a critical examination must begin from the fact that capital itself has no inherent dependence on or affinity to political freedom. Capital is a process oriented to the creation of profit, not to the attainment of freedom. Political goals of any kind, conservative or liberal, enter into the considerations of capital only insofar as they affect the M-C-M' circuit. The normal relation of capital to state power is therefore pragmatic, gladly accepting the use of military, bureaucratic, legislative, or other state interventions when they

---

*One must note "potentially." Capitalist governments can also apply direct coercive power and have done so on many occasions, as during national emergencies, crippling strikes, etc.

12. Giddens, *Historical Materialism.* For a bold attempt to describe a socialist structure that would provide such bulwarks to liberty see Branko Horvat, *The Political Economy of Socialism* (Armonk, N.Y.: M. E. Sharpe, Inc., 1982).

favor accumulation, resisting them when they do not. To put it differently, capitalists have no interests *as capitalists* in promoting the cause of freedom. They are indeed more likely to have opposed interests, insofar as freedom may create subversive attitudes toward the regime of capital, although it needs to be said that on occasion capitalists have espoused liberties even when these threatened their economic interests.*

The same weak linkage between the nature of capital and the defense of freedom is to be found when we consider the kinds of dangers against which the ramparts of property presumably protect the individual. These dangers are described as the pressures of state-imposed conformity that destroy the individual's capacity for independence and self-development. Yet it could surely be argued that the pressures of the marketplace and of the ethos of capitalism also erode these capacities profoundly—perhaps even *as* profoundly—although not so dramatically or coercively as the interventions of the state. With regard to these economic pressures, the presence of a separate economic realm is a port of entry rather than a defensive barrier. As we have seen, however, disciplinary forces arising within the economic sphere are not considered to be "political" in their function. They thereby escape the critical gaze of political liberalism that perceives the presence of one kind of freedom under capitalism and is blind to the absence of another kind.

---

*I believe it also needs to be said that many of those who have argued on behalf of capitalism because of its connection with freedom have shown scant interest when free speech, academic liberty, or racial or sexual discrimination are under attack.

One last instance of the ideological interpretation of the problem is afforded by sharp differences in the idea of the "rights" that apply to each realm. It is universally considered to be an infringement on the rights of citizens if they cannot cast a vote on the determination of national or local affairs. No such infringement is felt, however, when these same citizens are denied the opportunity to cast a vote on the determination of the affairs of the company that employs them. So too, it is an elemental proposition of democracy that every voting citizen has the right to cast but one vote, whereas it is an equally elemental proposition of capitalism that every market participant may rightly cast as many votes as his or her wealth permits. The latter vote taking place in the economy, it is once again excused from the judgment of the polity.

None of this is meant as a carping critique of the ideology of political liberalism, much less of the freedoms whose affinity for capitalism it seeks to explain. The partial freedoms of capitalism represent a political attainment that far exceeds that of precapitalist civilizations, as well as of existing self-proclaimed Marxist socialisms. Political and intellectual liberties are perhaps the greatest bourgeois civilizational triumphs. Nevertheless they *are* bourgeois triumphs; and the ideology that tends to depict them in absolute terms becomes evident when we reflect not only on the limitations but the definitions of the freedoms that have been won.

A final matter deserves to be raised under the general rubric of the ideology of politics in a regime of capital. It concerns the nature of rulership itself, perhaps the foundational concept of political life. Within capitalism—at least in principle—the state retains the means of violence, and the economy must content itself with the persuasions of economic pressure. How is it possible, then, to speak of the capitalist class as "ruling," when it lacks the historic prerequisite for rulership?

In this much-debated issue, I find useful Immanuel Wallerstein's conception of a "universal" class.[13] In stratified societies, Wallerstein argues, there is normally one, and only one group that is aware of itself as a class. This does not mean it has an awareness of any oppressive, exploitative, or "domineering," role vis-à-vis other "classes." It means, rather, that one group alone feels itself to be the embodiment of the spirit and mission of the society that in fact it dominates. This "universal" class, embracing within its self-conception the whole of society, is the ruling class. In Hegel's terms, it is the only class that exists not merely *"an sich"*—by virtue of objective circumstances—but *"für sich"*—by virtue of its shared sense of place and mission.

It is precisely the presence or absence of such a sense of deeply-felt and universal authority—an authority that needs neither apology nor defense—that separates the idea of class from that of estates, elites, power groups, and the like. This applies with particular cogency to the case of capitalism's ruling class. We have just noted that this class does not itself possess the means of violence as it does those of production, and it is a familiar fact that in the fissured and bifurcated realms of the capitalist system the

---

13. Immanuel Wallerstein, *The Modern World-System*, Vol. I, pp. 351–52.

top class is subdivided into estate-like subgroups. Thus Branko Horvat, the distinguished Yugoslav economist, describes the uppermost stratum of capitalism as follows:

[In] capitalism four different and separate functional groups have been established. One of them is involved in business, while the remaining three manage state affairs. They are: business executives, politicians, public administrators, characteristically called public servants; and military personnel. Within each group a small elite exercises control. . . . Thus, in modern capitalist societies four functional elites—top businessmen, political leaders, high-level civil servants, and military commanders—comprise the ruling class. . . . [14]

What this acute description lacks is an explanation of how or why these contending groups, in Horvat's own words, comprise a "ruling class." The answer is the same as that which normally bound the rivalrous estates of seventeenth- and eighteenth-century absolutist society to a single principle of what a universal class should represent. In the second case the principle was that of a monarchy wielding traditional and inherent rights of blood and lineage. In the case of Horvat's contending elites, it is the principle of a regime wielding the rights of capital.

Needless to say, the rights and privileges of all ruling classes can be amended by the intrusion of other allied, but differently oriented, factions, and on occasion can be suspended, as by a coup d'état. Usually the regime is resumed under new management; very rarely, one ruling class will be displaced by another embodying a wholly different conception of its role as the universal class—the two major

---

14. Horvat, *Political Economy of Socialism,* p. 68.

instances in modern history being the victory of the bourgeoisie itself during the eighteenth and nineteenth centuries, and the dramatic overthrow of the Tsarist bourgeoisie in the Russian Revolution. But such coups and revolutions are easily compatible with Wallerstein's conception of a single universal class as the norm. In this regard it is surely striking that not one of Horvat's contending groups —not the military, not the civil service, and not the politicians—would propose the advancement of its own interest —military force, bureaucratic entrenchment, or simply "politics"—as constituting the fundamental purpose of capitalist society. On the other hand, the capital-owning class, *with the concurrence of all,* asserts the encouragement of "economic growth" or "private enterprise" or "freedom"—meaning the bounded freedoms of capitalism —to be precisely that. It is in this sense that the capital-owning class is the universal class of capitalism, ruling by historic authority, for which weapons are not ordinarily a necessity.

## IV

A third general aspect of capitalist ideology remains to be examined. This is its "culture," that portmanteau word covering the diffuse values, the styles of art and thought, unconscious customs, and general outlook of the system, apart from those aspects we have singled out for examination under the rubrics of economics and political liberalism. From the beginning, bourgeois culture has been extraordinarily rich, brilliant, and diverse, not to be reduced to a single strand. Of all aspects of life in a capitalist society it is the least dependent on the regime of capital, the least directly traceable in its origins to economic life in general. This flowering culture has not been itself the direct product of the capitalist class but has rather arisen partly under its patronage or that of the state, and partly as an expression of opposition to the dominating role of capital. Nonetheless, no previous regime in history has stirred up or tolerated so rich, diverse, or critical a range of artistic and intellectual creativity. There are, of course, aspects of this "bourgeois" culture that bespeak their milieu, including most egregiously the commercialization of daily life of which I have spoken. But to compress the influence of capital on its culture to this aspect is to fail to appreciate the subtlety of the relationship of these two realms.

Hence I shall stress here another, more often overlooked element, before returning at the end to one last consideration of the direct imprint of the business world on the world of thought. The neglected side I wish to emphasize has to do with the bourgeois attitude toward nature. One aspect of the culture of most past civilizations strikes everyone who examines these extraordinarily diverse societies. This is their sacred view of the world. Whether in China or India, in Greece or Rome, the Americas or Africa, the earth is seen by earlier civilizations as peopled with spirits and living presences, suffused with an animism that inhabits every rock as well as every living thing. The world is endowed with the capacity for suffering and rejoicing, for vengeance and for beneficence. It exists to be cajoled, propitiated, rewarded, and thanked, not to be abused, invaded, violated, or ignored.[15]

---

15. See, for example, Fustel de Coulanges, *The Ancient City* (New York: Doubleday, n.d.), Book I.

There is a striking departure from this animistic view in the Judeo-Christian tradition, which from Genesis on, bids man to seize and shape, appropriate and subdue nature for human purposes alone. Nature is therefore desacralized and objectified, making it possible, in Lynn White's words, to exploit nature in a "mood of indifference to the feelings of natural objects."[16] This reification of the natural world long predates the rise of capitalism, but it provides a milieu that encouraged the rational view characteristic of the capitalist universal calculus. In turn the nascent strands of capitalist relationships and beliefs strengthened the depersonalization of the natural environment. Max Weber has pointed to the "disenchanted" frame of mind essential for the operation of a capitalist system, where all elements of the situation are reduced, as far as possible, to the purely abstract considerations of income statements and balance sheets.[17]

Perhaps the most striking aspect of this desacralization affects the conception of labor itself, wrenched free of its traditional social and psychological meanings and reduced to general capacities for motion and performance that enable it to be utilized exactly as if it were a versatile, but sometimes balky, machine. There are, of course, immediate motives of self-interest that press capital to ignore every aspect of a work force except its latent labor power, but these motives receive support from, and lend support to, a view that reduces the objects in the material world to atoms and particles, propelled or held in place by

---

16. Lynn White, *Machina Ex Deo: Essays in the Dynamics of Western Civilization* (Cambridge, Mass.: M.I.T. Press, 1968), p. 86.

17. Max Weber, *Economy and Society* (New York: Oxford University Press, 1947), p. 158f.

"forces" capable of being described by mathematics but no longer by art or imagery.

Science thus becomes an ideology—that is, an explanatory view of the world. Despite its vaunted "positivist" approach and its shunning of truth by revelation, it nonetheless fills a social requirement indistinguishable from religion. Science is not ideological in the sense of an avowal of social values, or an overt partisanship for social interests. Its ideological aspect lies rather in the function played by its deepest conception—an indifferent and inert matter as the ultimate stuff of reality. It thus provides a world view compatible with, and needed by, that required for the limitless invasion of the world for the purpose of surplus accumulation. Capitalism would be impossible in a sacralized world to which men would relate with awe and veneration, just as such attitudes cannot arise in a society in which exchange value has reduced to a common denominator all use-values. Capitalism requires and engenders a belief in the indifference of "nature" to the operations performed on it by man, a point of view epitomized by the scientific outlook. The culture of capitalism thus expresses a voracious, even rapacious, attitude toward the material world—a point of view that would be impossible if that world were portrayed as "mother" Nature. The ideological function of science is to delegitimize this animistic view, replacing it with the much more powerful view of nature as object, the obedient servant and uncomplaining treasury of man.

I must make clear, as with the matter of economics, that the usefulness of science as an ideology for capitalism does not imply that it could not serve another master. It is not the sober procedures of science that have their unique affinity for the regime of capital, any more than the matter-of-fact realities of economics to which all efforts to improve modern material existence must have recourse. The aspect of science that capitalism seizes upon is the reduction of the universe to an array of units of energy that can be legitimately used for any purpose whatsoever. The purpose for which the regime of capital uses them is a source of inexhaustible surplus to be gathered by the perpetual motion of M-C-M'. Marshall Berman has projected vividly the image of a world in which this perpetual motion machine runs without inhibition:

If we look behind the sober scenes that the members of our bourgeoisie create, and see the way they really work and act, we see that these solid citizens would tear down the world if it paid.

Even as they frighten everyone with fantasies of proletarian rapacity and revenge, they themselves, through their inexhaustible dealing and developing, hurtle masses of men, materials and money up and down the earth, and erode or explode the foundations of everyone's lives as they go. Their secret—a secret they have managed to keep even from themselves—is that, behind their façades, they are the most violently destructive ruling class in history. . . .[18]

As Berman points out, it is Marx himself who first perceives this whirlwind energy with its threat of self-annihilation: in the *Manifesto* he and Engels describe modern bourgeois society as having "conjured up such mighty means of production and exchange" that it is "like

---

18. Marshall Berman, *All That Is Solid Melts into Air* (New York: Simon & Schuster, 1982), p. 100.

the sorcerer who can no longer control the powers of the underworld that he had called up by his spirits." What Marx does not remark, however, and Berman does not explore, is that the forces of production alone were not enough to allow capitalism to achieve its material triumphs. It needed also the "permission" of nature itself, a permission that could only be achieved by draining nature of its vast animistic sensibility, leaving behind an uncomplaining grid of space and time.

One further issue requires our attention before leaving the immense subject of "culture" as ideology. This brings us back to the problem of the impact of the regime of capital on the commodification of life—the systematic search for aspects of daily existence that can be incorporated within the M-C-M' circuit. This aspect of capitalist culture has been so widely noted and deplored that it seems unnecessary to add to the many critical words that have already written.[19] I would note instead another consequence of commodification that affects the culture of capitalism in ways that are more benign, though perhaps ultimately more destructive. This is the tendency of the regime of capital to regard *ideas* as commodities, so that it becomes a characteristic of bourgeois culture that the most outrageous—indeed, even overtly subversive—

---

19. I refer, nevertheless, to a few commentaries of unusual value. Anthony Giddens discusses the commodification of time (following Mumford) as a penetration by capital of crucial and neglected importance (*Historical Materialism*, Ch. 6). Erich Kahler (citing copiously from Fromm) gives a stinging analysis of the commodification of perceptions in *The Tower and the Abyss* (New York: Braziller, 1976), p. 93f. Finally, I mention again Michael Schudson's *Advertising: The Uneasy Persuasion* for a penetrating analysis of a consumer society.

books, games, motion pictures, art, or even style can quickly become absorbed ("coopted") by the system.

There is, of course, a countertrend to this commercially motivated acquiesence in, or indifference to, ideas. A general suspicion of, or self-imposed censorship of, anti-capitalist views provides a considerable degree of protection for the system, the power of capital serving as the same indirect source of discipline in the ideological world as it does in the allocation of scarce resources. Nonetheless, no social formation is without its means of self-defense against hostile or subversive ideas. What is striking about capitalism is the willingness to accept potentially subversive influences once they are denatured by becoming commodities. Thus anti-capitalist or anti-bourgeois books become "best sellers"; essentially critical games such as Monopoly or even Class Struggle are sold with much the same indifference to their content as Parcheesi; anti-establishment motion pictures are promoted with the same zest as films of economic piety, providing they have box-office appeal; anti-bourgeois art or styles—the fad for workingmen's clothes, for instance—are eagerly embraced as successful items for merchandising without the smallest awareness of, or concern for, their symbolic rejection of the values of the larger culture.

All this, of course, is part of the extraordinary richness and creativity of capitalist culture. At the same time it is necessary to comment on two aspects of this cultural face of capitalism. The first is that the extraordinary tolerance for heretical, skeptical, or disconcerting thought and cultural activity is a direct consequence of the desacralization we have emphasized as the central characteristic of capitalist ideology. It should be noted, for instance, that in general the tolerance for subversive thought is much greater within the sphere of capital itself than in the realm of government. Lèse majesté remains a legal offense, but lèse capitale has not yet become one.

Second, it is only *because* ideas are commodities that they can be so lightly and indifferently regarded. A culture based on sacred beliefs would have great difficulty in tolerating continuous threats to the validity and sanctity of its world view. As I have written elsewhere, this poses serious challenges for those who believe that "socialism" will be naturally compatible with the intellectual freedom that is capitalism's remarkable achievement—an achievement whose basis is, I think, a devotion not to John Stuart Mill's faith in liberty but rather to the all-too-revealing depiction of the contest of thoughts as a *marketplace* of ideas. I do not wish to ally myself with those who equate capitalism with enlightenment, or socialism in whatever form as inseparable from intellectual repression: the realities are more complicated than that. But it is important to reflect on the cushioning protection afforded to intellectual life under capitalism precisely because it is in its nature that it develops a complex ideological system; and it is necessary as well to ponder the form in which a more ideologically unified society would cope with intellectual dissent.[20]

This absorptive capacity of capitalism is, however, also a weakness for the system. The ceaseless outpouring of

---

20. See my *Marxism: For and Against,* pp. 167–69. For a description of the manner in which a unified ideology is formed in a religious society that bears many resemblances to a communitarian form of socialism, see Gertrude Enders Huntington, "Children of the Hutterites," *Natural History,* February 1981.

commodified culture, the cacaphony of ten thousand books, magazines, and television impressions is in the end a recipe for confusion rather than enlightenment. Where Whirl is king, anarchy is ruler. Capitalism's view of its own existence, unlike that of all other social formations, lacks the basis of a religious certainty, the granite in which other world views are imprisoned but on which they can build with utter confidence. If science is capitalism's closest substitute for a religious underpinning for its historic life history, it is also the fact that science is at its core only a general method, itself in a constant state of flux.

The ideological aspect of the culture of capitalism, then, is not merely the imprint that the imperatives of capital leave on its productions. Rather, in parallel to the narrowness of the capitalist economic vision, and of its political conceptions, what is notable about its cultural outlook is the compression of the realm of culture itself. It is part of the nature of capitalism that the circuit of capital has no intrinsic moral dimension, no vision of art or idea aside from the commodity form in which it is embodied. In this setting, ideas thrive but morality languishes, and the regime of capital becomes the breeding ground for an explosion of ideational and esthetic creations that conceal beneath their brilliance the absence of an organizing moral force.

# 6

# The Logic of Capitalist Development

UP TO NOW we have spoken mainly of the nature of capitalism—the institutions and beliefs that endow the social formation with its magnetic character. In considering this nature we have been at pains to emphasize one primary consideration. It is that the social formation of capitalism, like that of all others save only primitive society, is at bottom a system of class domination and mass acquiescence. That which distinguishes capitalism from other social formations is not the fact of its hierarchical character but its unique form, in which the drive for power and domination becomes sublimated into the desire to accumulate capital, and in which the expression of subordinate status is manifested through the acceptance of market and property relations. The regimes of capital display a great variety of forms, from the enlightened countries of northern Europe to the repressive Union of South Africa, but all—even those that speak of themselves as "socialist"—still maintain the institution of capital as the dominating element in their social structures. However hedged about or surrounded by advanced political and ideological ways and views, the accumulation of capital remains the life force of these nations, the center not only of their economic but of their social and political life.

It follows, then, that at the deepest level the logic of capitalism must also express the imperatives of accumulation. The fundamental force that drives the system through history is its search for profit—a search on whose outcome hinges the historical fate of the social formation as a whole. This relentless and insatiable process, into whose genesis and ramifications we have inquired at length, therefore sets into motion the central tendencies of the system. The capitalist path takes different turnings at different periods of history, and the paths of capitalist nations by no means run along exactly parallel tracks; and yet in all its variations, the trajectory of capitalism is immediately recognizable as a movement guided by the imperious need for profit—indeed, as a movement incomprehensible without an awareness of this central element of its nature.

As I said at the outset, the dynamics of this logic have been the main research objective of all the great economists. The works of Smith and Mill and Marx and Keynes and Schumpeter describe the outcome of a grand drama of accumulation that all recognize as constitutive of, and inseparable from, the innermost principle of being of the system they are studying. That these scenarios reflect differing empirical observations and conceptual perspectives is obvious enough. Less noticed is that the scenarios also embrace a common framework of basic assumptions. From Smith to Schumpeter, the great works of political economy recognize that the vital accumulation process hinges on the ability of a capitalist class to extract profit from the system. All further understand that this ability depends on the legitimacy of property rights in the means of production. All also understand that these rights require a mutually supportive division of functions between the realm of business and that of the state—a division of functions that takes for granted the priority of accumulation as a necessary condition for a stable social order. These universally recognized preconditions for accumulation constitute a tacit delineation of what we have called the "regime" of capital—that is, the depiction of capitalism as a social formation in which the accumulation of capital becomes the organizing basis for sociopolitical life.

In addition, all the major scenarios are dramas of social as well as material evolution. Growth and change lie at their hearts. In particular, the great economists emphasize that the accumulation process is an agency for social, not just economic, change and that one of its main effects is to alter, for better or worse, the fortunes of the social classes of the system.

Finally, all the great scenarios envisage the regime as having a bounded future. Its span of life cannot be precisely predicted, but its eventual demise or supersession by another social order is universally foreseen. Adam Smith describes the system as reaching a plateau, when the accumulation of riches will be "complete," bringing about a deep and lengthy decline. John Stuart Mill expects the momentary arrival of a "stationary state," when accumulation will cease and capitalism will become the staging ground for a kind of associationist socialism. Marx anticipates a sequence of worsening crises produced by the internal contradictions of accumulation—each crisis clearing away the obstacles of the moment but hastening the day when the system will no longer be able to manage its self-generated tensions. Keynes thought the future would require a "somewhat comprehensive socialization of investment"; Schumpeter thought it would evolve into managerial socialism.[1]

This broad theme unquestionably raises the crucial aspect of the logic of capital, namely its capacity to survive in the face of the obstacles and difficulties that accumulation creates. Despite their general consensus with respect to the long-term future, however, the generalized narratives of the worldly philosophers have little to tell us about the present or the foreseeable future. Nothing like a timetable exists for the expected life span of the system—Schumpeter, who predicts the system's passing, cautions that "in these things, a century is a 'short run.' "[2] There is no agreement on the proper measure of the vitality of the system. Perhaps most striking of all, a hundred years after Marx's enunciation of a "law" of the falling tendency of the rate of profit, no conclusive evidence exists as to whether the rate of profit has shown a secular decline or not.[3]

Thus an attempt to investigate the logic of the system

---

1. Smith, *Wealth of Nations,* p. 111; Mill, *Principles of Political Economy,* pp. 738,752f.; Karl Marx, *Capital,* III, Part 3; John Maynard Keynes, *The General Theory of Employment, Interest and Money* (New York: Harcourt Brace & Co., 1936), Ch. 24, p. 378; Joseph Schumpeter, *Capitalism, Socialism, and Democracy* (New York: Harper & Row, 1946), Chs. 12, 13.

2. Schumpeter, *Capitalism,* p. 163.

3. See the discussion in the *Cambridge Journal of Economics,* June 1978 and March 1980.

in terms of its life expectancy yields no more than an anticipation of its eventual decline, an expectation of little use in understanding the present or the near-term future —indeed, an expectation that may cause grave mischief if plans are laid for the system's quick demise without heed to the possibility that Schumpeter's calculations with respect to the "short run" might prove to be correct.

There is, however, another aspect of the logic of the system, also present although less prominent in the work of the great economists. This is the effect of accumulation in bringing about structural changes *within* the system—changes that alter the manner in which capital pursues its unchanging goal. This logic will not come directly to grips with the question of how long profits can be won, a matter that must ultimately be decided by the changing balance of class power—Marx's "class struggle"; by the ebb and flow of technological opportunity; by the fortunes of war and conquest; and other such largely imponderable factors. The logic of structural change will nonetheless shed some light on the evolving shape and form of the social formation—the changes in flesh and bone, so to speak, that are forced on the body social by the inner metabolism of M-C-M'. From these changes we may yet learn something that bears on the larger logic of the capitalist prospect itself.

## II

The logic of structural transformation comes about as the direct outcome of the manner in which capital is generally amassed once the transition to an industrial capitalism has been made. This takes the form of the building up of "fixed" capital—machines and equipment, factories and buildings, transportation and power networks, and in our own day, research facilities.

Capital seeks to amass these fixed investments for several reasons.[4] One is that they strengthen the hand of capital against labor because machinery greatly increases the productivity of labor, as exemplified by the assembly line. This enables individual capitals to increase their profitability, at least for a time, because the cost of labor per unit of output declines. A second reason is associated with the same increase in productivity. The ability to cut costs is a primary means by which firms seek to invade the markets of their competitors or to stave off competition from others. Third, fixed capital is usually necessary in order to bring new products on line, where they can seek the "rents" of scarcity.

The structural logic of accumulation therefore begins from the powerful tendency of capital to develop its productive forces—a tendency we are familiar with as an integral aspect of the M-C-M' circuit. With this enhanced ability, however, come two associated effects that undermine and disrupt that self-same circuit. The first arises from the effect of additional fixed capital in "crowding out" labor. From a Marxian analytic viewpoint this progressively erodes the basis from which surplus value can be extracted, thereby setting into motion the famous tendency of the falling rate of profit. Even from a conventional view, which does not recognize the existence of surplus value, the crowding out of labor by machinery

---

4. See "Economic Crises" by Anwar Shaikh, in Bottomore, ed., *A Dictionary of Marxist Thought* (Cambridge, Mass.: Harvard University Press, 1983), pp. 138–143.

introduces difficulties in the form of a threat of technological unemployment.

Second, and no less important from both a Marxist and a non-Marxist perspective, is the effect of fixed capital in augmenting the physical capacity of individual industries without any coherent plan for dovetailing their outputs. In Marx's terminology the ensuing tendency for a mismatch of supply and demand aggravates the "anarchy" of a capitalist economy. For other economists, it is the source of those recurrent saturations of individual markets that can bring enormous economic damage when the markets are of major importance, such as the over-building of the railways at the end of the nineteenth century.

Thus accumulation becomes the cause of a clash between enhanced productive capacity on the one hand, and the limited adaptive capacities of the market mechanism on the other. The logic embodies a conflict between what Marx calls the "unconditional development" of society's productive genius and the "limited purpose" of capital as a vehicle for the attainment of that productive genius, the limitation being that capital is a process oriented to profit, not to social well-being. This is the final contradiction to which we turn in *Capital.* After tracing the labyrinthine path of the circuit of accumulation in great detail, Marx writes in Volume III, "The *true barrier* of capital accumulation is *capital* itself," a succinct if cryptic description of the inherent tensions in what I am calling the structural logic of the system.[5]

---

5. Marx *Capital,* III, p.358. See also Wood, "Marxism and the Course of History," *New Left Review,* September/October 1984, esp. pp. 102–3.

Shortly we must attempt to trace the developmental logic of capitalism in greater detail, moving from the abstract, timeless representation of a contradiction between productive expansion and social restriction to a depiction of this tension in the actual configurations and patterns of historical capitalism. In doing so, however, we encounter a new problem. It is that the developmental logic of the system does not unfold in a single uninterrupted flow but rather takes place in distinct stages or periods. At our level of Olympian observation these long-lasting stages might be likened, at least metaphorically, to the youth, young adulthood, maturity, and old age into which the early historians divided the chronology of past kingdoms.

I have set out these stages (without such tendentious titles) on the chart on pages 150–52. The chart is segmented into sections that highlight aspects of the political and ideological as well as the economic realms, some of which I will explore in some detail, others of which I include only to round out the general character of the periods into which the array is subdivided. For what is crucial in this presentation are not the elements that we trace from one stage to the next—elements that are highly compressed and unavoidably arbitrary to a degree—but rather the guiding principle by which periodization itself is determined.

Here I follow the works of Ernest Mandel and of David Gordon, theorists of "long waves" in capitalism. These are roughly twenty-five-year-long periods of buoyant expansion, followed by equally protracted periods of sluggish growth, that reveal their stimulating or retarding presence in many aspects of capitalist performance, most importantly in the relative length of boom years versus slump years in the "normal" seven-to-eleven-year business cycles over which the long waves extend.

From Mandel I take the conception of these long swings as the expression of deep-rooted changes in the contest of forces that determine the prevailing profitability of the system—in short, the "class struggle" that regulates the division of the social product into the share going to capital and that going to labor. This approach has the virtue of historic specificity, since Mandel emphasizes that political and technological configurations will vary from one long boom to the next. What it lacks, however, is the ability to account for the long duration of the swells and falls themselves. Here Gordon's analysis provides a useful supplement by emphasizing the influence of the "social structure" of accumulation, the overall milieu within which accumulation takes place. Gordon places particular stress on the mode of deploying labor within industrial enterprise, but he recognizes also the importance of competitive strategies, business/government relationships, and the like. The extended long wave can then be envisaged as the effect of a given social structure on the ability to amass capital. Typically a structure will encourage investment until the opportunities for expansion within a given framework of social and institutional constraints are exhausted. Thereupon pressure accumulates to create a new set of arrangements—labor deployment, market organization, government regulation, etc.—better able to foster the profitable engagement of labor. It is therefore a periodicity whose timing reflects the inertia of

## A HISTORICAL SCHEMA OF THE LOGIC OF CAPITALIST DEVELOPMENT

| | 1760–1848 | 1848–1893 | 1893–1941 | 1941– |
|---|---|---|---|---|
| **STRUCTURE OF THE ACCUMULATION PROCESS** | | | | |
| *Size of typical capitals* | small scale (single plant) | moderate scale (multi-building, single-product) | national scale (multi-location, multi-product) | international scale (multi-industry) |
| *Organization of capitals* | proprietary or partnership | family corporation | managerial bureaucracy | state participation |
| *Strategy of M-C-M'* | displacement of precapitalist sector | expansion of domestic and foreign markets through cost reduction and commodification | | global positioning; technological development |
| *Technology* | pre-industrial machinery | industrial machinery | | science-made machinery |
| *Labor process* | division of tasks with "proletarianized" labor | assembly-line tasks with "homogenized" labor | | science-based tasks, supervisory labor |
| *Competition (mutual encroachment)* | buffered by slow expansion and precapitalist sector | increased by mechanized production | | intensified by international and technological forces |
| *Defensive tactics of private capitals* | none | pools; later trusts and vertical integration | mergers, oligopoly | use of state power |

## FUNCTIONS OF THE ECONOMIC AND POLITICAL REALMS

| | | | |
|---|---|---|---|
| *Economic functions of the political realm* | | | |
| DOMESTIC | widening provision of infrastructure (transportation, education, science) | regulation of markets | demand management, state planning |
| FOREIGN | tariff policies, minor commercial wars | direct military imperialism | economic hegemony; international economic arrangements |
| *Political functions of the economic realm* | repressive discipline through market pressures | consensual discipline through rising mass consumption | increasing labor cooptation by management |
| **ASPECTS OF IDEOLOGY** | | | |
| *The economic system as explained by economics* | means of social accumulation | means for individual advancement | means for efficiency and freedom |
| *Liberal view of class struggle (in Europe)* | labor regarded as "dangerous class" | labor accepted within regime, but still considered as potentially socialist | labor interest seen as identical with regime |
| *Role of science as understood by the regime of capital* | no relation to accumulation | useful adjunct for accumulation | essential for accumulation |

*(Table continued)*

## GENERAL CHARACTERISTICS OF THE CRISIS PERIOD

| | 1760–1848 | 1848–1893 | 1893–1941 | 1941– |
|---|---|---|---|---|
| *Crisis years* | 1800–48 | 1873–93 | 1929–41 | 1973–(?) |
| *Economic aspects* | destruction of precapitalist sector | market instability | generalized depressions | state intervention |
| *Ideological and political aspects* | labor unrest countered by repression | socialist movements countered by "economic patriotism" | | deflection of disaffections onto the state |

adjustment—a "generational" explanation of the duration of long swings.[6]

This means that each period within the chart must be conceived as a snapshot of *processes,* caught in an instant of time—processes that are impelling the entire system in the direction of a general impasse indicated at the conclusion of the developmental logic in each period. The individual features within periods are therefore typically more representative of its physiognomy at the end of the period than at the beginning. I have divided the historic canvas into four periods as to whose distinctive character there is little controversy. What is controversial, I repeat, is the assumption that each period is defined and climaxed by its terminal crisis. The idea of a historic accumulation process, manifesting itself at first in a burst of newly released energy and gradually encountering the limitations of its social structure, will nonetheless provide the basis on which our discussion will proceed.

I will not therefore spend any time on the statistics that demonstrate the length or amplitude of these rhythmic surges, nor refer, except in passing, to the specific industries or commodities that play crucial roles in leading each upward movement. My interest, rather, is in revealing a characteristic structure within which capitalist growth takes place in each of its periods. The chart is therefore a

---

6. Ernest Mandel, *Late Capitalism* (London: New Left Books), Ch. 4 and *Long Waves of Capitalist Development* (New York: Cambridge University Press, 1980); David Gordon, Up and Down the Long Roller Coaster," in U.S. Capitalism in Crisis (New York: Union for Radical Political Economics, 1978) and Gordon, Richard Edwards, and Michael Reich, *Segmented Work, Divided Workers* (New York: Cambridge University Press, 1982), Ch 2. They are not responsible for the "generational" interpretation of their thesis.

heuristic more than an analytic device. It does not purport to show how the system is catapulted from the terminal crisis of one period to the fresh configuration of the next. It aims to present no more than the setting within which we shall attempt to find a logic of accumulation that changes its manifestations but not its fundamental nature from one period to the next.

## III

We begin with the period of nascent industrial capitalism, the era already sufficiently well formed so that Adam Smith could delineate its features in *The Wealth of Nations*. I shall not recapitulate here the features of that social structure of accumulation, leaving to the reader to reconstruct its portrait from the first column of the matrix. The underlying logic is, of course, set into motion in the activities where the accumulation process is outlined, and it is there that we accordingly direct our attention first.

It is Smith himself who gives us the Ariadne's thread into that process when, in the opening pages of the *Wealth,* he introduces us to a "small" pin manufactory where ten men, "indifferently" equipped with machinery, are able to produce forty-eight thousand pins a day, whereas (Smith tells us) each man, if he had "wrought separately and independently . . . certainly could not . . . have made twenty, perhaps not one pin in a day."[7] This is the famous principle of the division of labor, the driving

---

7. Smith, *Wealth of Nations,* pp. 14–15.

force of the accumulation process in Smith's scenario, whose power depends partly on the militarylike pace and discipline of the work force, partly on the increase in individual dexterity that is the result of specialized and repetitive tasks, and most of all on the supplementation of human strength and precision by the use of machinery in the production process. If we generalize the extraordinary leverage imparted to production by its mechanization, we discover immediately the source of the impetus to which we commonly give the name the "Industrial" Revolution —in fact, the first of a succession of technological revolutions.

Looking back on this initial period with the benefit of hindsight, what strikes us is not merely the encouragement given to production by the early mechanization and division of labor but the equally important function played by the existing economic structure in *moderating* its disruptive force. This was the consequence of two aspects of the period: one technological, one social. The technological aspect was the product of the still undeveloped character of its technology and application. The Watt steam engine and the Arkwright waterframe were essentially hand-built mechanisms, without standardized and interchangeable parts or subcomponents. The staggering increase in productivity of Smith's manufactory, from a few pins to 4,800 pins per man per day, was not realized in a single bound from artisanate to manufactory but came as the result of a process of expansion that proceeded one man and one machine at a time: in the 1830s, more than a half-century after the introduction of the textile mill, two-thirds of the mills in England still employed less than fifty workers, and in the United States, according to the Census of Manufactures of 1869, the average number of workers in "manufacturing" establishments was still less than ten.[8]

Thus the potentially disruptive impact of expanding capital was held in check by the primitive character of its equipment and organization. Equally important was a social attribute of the period—namely, the existence of a large precapitalist sector against which the output from the new manufactories could be directed. Handicrafts became the target of the mills, with the well-known result of their virtual elimination, first in England in the early decades of the nineteenth century, later in India. The same destruction also occurred, although with much less harmful social results, in the United States, where the output of homespuns in New York State fell from almost ten yards per capita in 1825 to barely more than a quarter of a yard thirty years later.[9]

As a result, competition for the nascent capitalist firms assumed the form of a mild disciplinary force—the source, Smith writes, of "good management"[10]—bringing about a uniform rate of profit and a flexible adaptation of outputs to demand but minimizing the violent consequences that would figure so importantly in later periods of the system. For a considerable time, the new power of the forces of

---

8. David Landes, *The Unbound Prometheus* (New York: Cambridge University Press, 1969) p. 120; *Historical Statistics of the United States* (Washington, D.C., Bureau of Census, 1975) Series P 1, 4, 5.

9. George Taylor, *The Transportation Revolution* (New York: Holt, Rinehart & Winston, 1962), p. 213.

10. Smith, *Wealth of Nations,* pp. 163–164.

production was therefore able to exert its effect on output with relatively small adverse effects on the values of existing capitals.

Far more dramatic was the impact of the emerging industrial mode of production on another social aspect of the system, the newly recruited "proletarianized" work force of unemployed or dispossessed men and women forced to accept the dreaded work of the mills for survival's sake. Smith believed that industrial employment would have a two-sided effect on working persons. He thought it would improve their material lot but injure their moral and intellectual well-being. Material conditions would improve, he argued, because the accumulation process would maintain a steady upward gradient, with real wages rising fast enough to better the workers' lot, but not so fast as to jeopardize profitability. Their moral fiber and intellectual acumen, on the other hand, would undergo a severe deterioration from an exposure to the same mechanized division of labor that was responsible for their more "liberal" wages. As Smith put it:

... The understandings of the greater part of men are necessarily formed by their ordinary employments. The man whose whole life is spent in performing a few simple operations . . . has no occasion to exert his understanding, or to exercise his invention in finding out expedients for removing difficulties which never occur. He naturally loses, therefore, the habit of such exertion, and generally becomes as stupid and ignorant as it is possible for a human creature to become. . . . [11]

---

11. Smith, *Wealth of Nations,* pp. 781–82.

Smith was incorrect on both accounts, and his error is of interest insofar as it helps define aspects of the social framework of his period. He was incorrect in anticipating a rise in the material well-being of the working class because he did not foresee the catastrophic effect of the proletarianization of the working force, with its ragged pauper apprentices, its Irish immigrants, displaced artisans, and dispossessed agricultural laborers. Wages did not rise in the tempered fashion that Smith expected but gradually declined from 1780 until about 1820, in some cases falling precipitously: Manchester weavers, who had enjoyed earnings of 15s to 20s per week in the 1790s, were reduced to 5s and 6s per week by 1800. The decline in wages was worsened by the near-collapse of urban living standards in the mill towns. Continental and English visitors were as appalled by Manchester as Frederick Engels: "Civilization works its miracles and civilized man is turned back almost into a savage," wrote Tocqueville on visiting the city.[12]

Smith's second and more significant error was his expectation that the working class would lose its "martial spirit" as well as its acumen, and would be reduced to a state of apathetic ignorance. That was not in fact the outcome. It was not apathy but anger that grew within the proletariat, evidenced at first in movements of religious dissent, then in episodes of machine breaking and factory burning and finally in mass protests and minor "revolts."

---

12. Wages from Phyllis Deane, *The First Industrial Revolution* (Cambridge: Cambridge University Press, 1965), pp. 146, 244. Tocqueville quote from Eric Hobsbawm, *Industry and Empire* (New York: Pantheon, 1968), pp. 67–68.

Between Waterloo and the Peterloo massacre, according to the English historian Asa Briggs, England was closer to a social revolution than at any time in her history.[13] Meanwhile, similar sentiments grew on the Continent, bursting out in the revolutions of 1848—revolutions that were put down with humiliating ease but that were capable nonetheless of conjuring up specters of social overturn to the reactionary governments of Europe and premature visions of an end to capital for radicals such as Marx and Engels.

The dynamics of early industrial expansion, at first encouraged by the presence of a vulnerable artisanate sector, later discouraged by the disappearance of that sector under the impact of industrial manufacturing itself; and the tensions of the class struggle, first overwhelmed by the squalor and discipline of the new industrial mode of life, later whetted and focused by it, together endow the early period of capitalism with the unmistakable aspects of a logic of accumulation. The logic is still parochial in its scope and muted in its impact, in that capitalism is mainly confined to a few nations and not even generalized throughout their economies. Nonetheless, the specific quality of capitalism's historic trajectory, manifest as a new mode of organizing production shaped by the drive for capital expansion, brings a two-sided effect—an encouragement to output and a disruption to economic and social life. Thus the stage is set for the intensification and magnification of these effects as the age

---

13. From Deane, *Industrial Revolution,* p. 247. See also E. P. Thompson, *The Making of the English Working Class* (New York: Pantheon, 1964), Ch. 16.

of "manufacture," as Marx called it, gives way in the second long wave to the age of what he called "machinofacture."

## IV

There is no mistaking the change that occupies the center of the stage in the next period. It is the enormous enlargement, intensification, and acceleration of the M-C-M' circuit, concentrated in the central portion of the process where labor power and raw materials are converted into finished commodities. What is important here are not merely the dramatic differences of technologies—the contrast between pins produced on hand presses and steel rails shot from rollers at forty miles per hour—but the accompanying differences in the size of work forces, up from troops of ten men to armies of five and ten thousand—and in the case of the largest corporations, over one hundred thousand men; in the extent of money capitals, no longer limited by the size of the fortune of a single proprietor or his partners but now amassed from the entire regime through the issuance of corporation shares and bonds; in the character of management and supervision, once concentrated in the abilities of a jack-of-all-trades entrepreneur and his trusted clerks, now parceled out among specialized functionaries, the bureaucrats of production and marketing, labor supervision and engineering, finance and bookkeeping. The technological impetus for the new boom was located in its machine-made machines and its universalization first of iron products, then of steel, but the larger change in the forces of production involved alterations in the organization of production as well as in its technical advance.

A central aspect of this reorganization was a marked change in the deployment of labor within the factory. As David Landes and others economic historians have noted, the use of labor in early capitalism, although often harshly repressive, was not particularly efficient. In the iron foundries, mines, machine shops, and of course in agriculture, the pace of labor was still set by men, not by machines. Periods of intensive activity were followed by periods of waiting around. The work itself resembled a congeries of craftlike tasks where simple mechanization assisted the workman, rather than a work flow where traditional barriers of craft played little or no role.[14]

This casual organization of labor was not compatible with mass production, which required that work effort be continuous and subject to much more management-directed discipline. The craftlike organization of tasks had therefore to be replaced by a "homogenized" labor force before the rhythms and speeds of mass-production technology could be fully applied. As Gordon, Edwards, and Reich have pointed out, the dramatic shift in the forces of production that played so crucial a role in defining the structure of accumulation in the middle periods of the system would not have been feasible without appropriate changes in the mode of labor deployment. This entailed the break-up of the semi-autonomous gang system, with its bosslike labor contractors, and the assertion of direct managerial prerogatives over the hours and conditions of labor. From this change in the position of the worker emerged the homogenization of a previously variegated labor force; and from the homogenization of labor came

---

14. Landes, *Unbound Prometheus,* p. 121.

the "drive system"—the fast pacing, routinization, and "scientific" management that were given their most articulate expression in the work of Frederick Taylor. The international acclaim given to Taylorism attests to its importance in changing the possibilities of the accumulation circuit. Even Lenin was an enthusiast for scientific management.[15]

The homogenization of labor enormously magnified the mutual impact of expanding capitals. Drive system labor forces and enormous assemblages of machinery hurled torrents of output against other capitals, transforming the process of mutual encroachment from a disciplinary to a destructive interaction. National corporations, with large sums invested in plant and equipment, had to "run full" (as Andrew Carnegie put it) to cover their heavy fixed costs, which, in the case of American railroads, amounted to as much as two-thirds of running costs.[16] Running full reduced unit costs for each firm, but the consequence of all firms running full was the continuous outbreak of unmanageable "cut-throat" competition, with rate wars among railroads and price wars among oil refineries and steel mills. With the gradual saturation of the market for rail lines, steel, and other mass commodities, competition—the stimulating source of "good management" lauded by Smith—became the source of the internecine war described by Marx. In 1873 lagging growth set off an irregu-

---

15. See Gordon, Edwards, and Reich, *Segmented Work,* p. 100f.; also Harry Braverman, *Labor and Monopoly Capital* (New York: Monthly Review Press, 1974), p. 12 and Ch. 4.

16. Alfred Chandler, Jr., *The Railroads* (New York: Harcourt, Brace & World 1965), p. 159.

lar twenty-year decline, at the end of which prices had fallen by two-thirds and the business failure rate had approximately doubled. Looking over the wreckage at the end of 1893, *Bradstreet* judged the crisis to have been the worst in eighty years.[17]

The enhanced productive powers of technology therefore greatly increased its disruptive powers. The immediately linked result was to be found in the measures of defense by which capitals sought to protect themselves against the onslaught. In the early period of limited mutual encroachment, there was essentially no effective means of defense, short-lived collusions aside. But the intensification of pressures during the era we are considering provoked increasingly effective reflexes. In Europe the main barrier to the destructive expansion of capitals became the open formation of cartels, common by the turn of the century, and a turning toward international protectionism. In the United States the defensive effort at first took the form of pools and agreements against price cutting—almost entirely ineffective; then of vertical integrations that sought to exclude market forces by maintaining the passage of commodities from raw to finished states *within* the firm; finally of trusts and mergers, culminating in the great merger wave at the turn of the century.[18]

The working-out of the structural logic is therefore easy to discover. The interplay of the forces of production and

---

17. Charles Hoffman, "The Depression of the '90s," *Journal of Economic History,* June 1956.

18. See Alfred Chandler, *The Visible Hand* (Cambridge, Mass.: Harvard University Press, 1977), esp. pp. 285f.

the reflexes of defense had as its outcome the centralization and concentration of capital. To take an illustrative case, in 1870, before the blows of the initial depression, there were 808 iron and steel mills in the United States. Thirty years later, when the storm had passed, there were 669 mills and the average capital per firm had increased from $150,000 to $383,000. On a broader basis we can note that whereas in 1897 there had been only 20 trusts, the Census of 1900 listed 185 "consolidations" with a total capitalization of $1.4 billion, and four years later the number had grown to 445, with a capitalization of over $20 billion.[19]

Thus an enormous change in scale dominates the period culminating in the 1890s, in part the result of unprecedented advances in technology, in part the consequence of defensive efforts to protect capitals against the very productive efficiency they had created. In the initial decades of the next period, this underlying logic now continued its effects in the setting of the massive industrial structure that emerged from the previous era. In this restructured setting, the economy came less and less to resemble a honeycomb of small enterprises, each relatively weak but collectively flexible, and more and more took on the attributes of a massive concatenation of beams and girder, each very strong but collectively rigid and interlocked.

The effect of this change was soon evident. The girdered structure became a means of transmitting disruptions

---

19. Census Reports, 12th Census, 1900 (Washington, D.C.: U.S. Census Office, 1902), Vol. X, Table i, p. 4; Harold Faulkner. *The Decline of Laissez Faire* (New York: Holt, Rinehart & Winston, 1962), p. 25. I am indebted to Laurence Malone for correcting Faulkner's figure for capitalization in 1900.

throughout the system far more powerfully than the honeycomb. Mismatches of supply and demand, poor sectoral interlocks, or decelerations of accumulation from saturated markets transmitted their shocks as from earthquake epicenters. In addition, the productivity effect of fixed capital now began to cut sharply into the employment base as fewer workers were required per ton or yard of output. From 1900 to 1929 output in the manufacturing industries tripled while employment only doubled.[20] Marx would undoubtedly have characterized the movement from the crisis period of the 1870s and 1880s to that of the 1930s as a shift from disproportionality—the poor dovetailing of outputs—to underconsumption—a disproportionality of income payments. From both causes, the common result was a growing tendency for systemwide breakdowns to appear in the M-C-M′ circuit. In place of a disorganization of markets there was a disorganization of large economic flows, until in the gigantic collapse of the 1930s real industrial growth was zero or negative for ten consecutive years. The same catastrophic effects were visible on the Continent (where the devastation of World War I must bear a portion of the blame), as well as in England, less physically damaged by the war, where unemployment exceeded 10 percent in every year but one from 1919 to 1939.

The late nineteenth-century destablizations of price warfare had been countered, as we have seen, by trustification and merger, and later by the "price leadership" of

---

20. *Historical Statistics of the United States* (Washington, D.C.: Bureau of the Census, 1972), p. 668, Series P 40 and p. 137, Series D 130.

oligopolistic industries and by government regulatory intervention. However effective these public and private efforts to mitigate the ferocity of price competition, they were without effect against failures that required the revitalization of the entire system, not just the repair of localized or partial failures. Such a revitalization necessitated the injection of purchasing power into the economy across all markets, and during the 1930s governments as different as the Popular Front in France, the Nazi and Fascist regimes in Germany and Italy, and the New Deal in America all sought to restore the accumulation process by using such measures under various ideological guises.

That which distinguished the response to the two periods of crisis was therefore the roles of the private and public realms in providing a mechanism of rescue for the system. The crisis of the late nineteenth century was resolved mainly by the spontaneous initiatives of the business community itself, symbolized in the efforts of Carnegie, Morgan, Rockefeller, and others to stabilize their industries through business amalgamations of one kind or another. The crisis of the 1930s was attacked quite differently. Business leaders were unable to mount an effective defense against a disruption of such magnitude, and the initiatives accordingly passed to government leaders and their advisors. It was this forced partial reunification of the realms of business and government that gave to the scenario of the third period its essential point of structural difference from the second. The defining climax of the period ending in the crisis of the end of the nineteenth century was the initial trustification of capitalism; that of the period ending in the 1930s was the initial statification of the system.

We cannot leave the middle periods of the system without some consideration of the political confrontations that were also part of their developmental logics. This is all the more important in that the polarization of classes that bulked so large in Marx's conception of capitalist dynamics now encountered an aspect of the accumulation process to which Marx paid, in retrospect, far too little attention. This was the ability of the regime of capital to win allegiance by conjuring up a source of "patriotism" from the accumulation process itself. The patriotism is that of economic affluence—the gratitude, or at least the support, of the retainer for a generous patron.

The economic patriotism of the periods in question followed considerably different paths in America and Europe. In the United States, where the initial experience of factory and urban life never plumbed English and European depths, the allegiance of the working class was at no time seriously in question. Despite the harsh manner in which homogenized labor was used in the steel mills and auto plants, despite terrible slums and continuous racial and ethnic oppressions, the momentum of American growth early won the basic adherence of its masses, and never lost it. As Werner Sombart put it, "All socialist utopias came to nothing on roast beef and apple pie."[21]

---

21. Werner Sombart, *Why Is There No Socialism In The United States?* (White Plains, N.Y.: International Arts and Sciences Press, 1976), pp. 109–110.

The basis of American "exceptionalism"—its unique failure to develop an anticapitalist political consciousness—was the product not merely of an absence of the embittering European experience but the presence of a widening stream of mass consumption goods that soon took on the powerful psychological appeal of prestige goods: fancy inexpensive clothes, mass-produced furniture, small home appliances, eventually even the symbolic automobile. Thus the political and ideological logic of American capitalism reflected its successful economic logic, and the economic logic in turn was able to draw support from the allegiance of its working classes. In this way, the advent of the "department" store, of "installment" buying, and of the enticements of advertising served as recuitment agencies for the regime.[22] What is remarkable is that the desire for "prestige goods" proved as effective in driving the system as the need for survival on which the power of property originally depended.

Things were considerably different in Europe. Engels complained toward the end of his life about the "embourgeoisement" of the English working class, but the revolutionary spirit of the 1840s, however chastened or ineffective, never ceased to be a lurking threat to the regime. The Paris Commune, the working-class uprisings in post-World War I Germany, the English General Strike of 1926, and, of deepest impact, the communist revolution in Russia in 1917, all presented incontrovertible evidence that socialist systems of belief posed a direct challenge to

---

22. See Stuart and Elizabeth Ewen, *Channels of Desire* (New York: McGraw-Hill, 1982).

the very principle of the regime of capital. This doubtless played its part in shaping the attitudes of the Europe bourgeoisie with respect to labor—at first openly viewed as a "dangerous class" to be put down, later grudgingly admitted to political participation but still regarded as harboring subversive sentiments. These attitudes contrasted sharply with those of American capitalists, who always believed the working class to be bourgeois at heart.

Yet, for all its turmoil and socialist rhetoric, the working class in Europe never in fact overthrew the regime of capital. No doubt this speaks in the first place for the sheer power of the state, usually massed on the side of capital, but it testifies as well to the success of a process of political accommodation in conjuring up some degree of working-class economic patriotism. Measures to underpin working-class consumption, such as pensions, health insurance, unemployment benefits, and family allowances, were already beginning to appear in Europe in the 1930s (and even earlier). Although these were not sufficient to generate a positive allegiance to the system comparable to that which it enjoyed in America, they served at least to reduce the level of antagonism to one that the regime could tolerate.

Thus on both sides of the Atlantic the middle periods ended with the terms of the class struggle unresolved but clarified. American capitalism based its success not alone on the strong economic momentum developed by the accumulation process but also on a climate of economic patriotism that effectively eliminated any direct challenge to the regime of capital itself. The great depression thereby struck at the very basis of domination by removing the buoyancy of rising consumption on which American capitalism rested its economic politics. In Europe a somewhat different challenge faced the regime. What the European economies required for their successful assertion of domination was an economic impetus that would duplicate that of the United States.

Political and economic logics in this way converged to a remarkable degree. An altered social structure of accumulation was needed both to counteract the massive breakdowns in the economic circuit and to engender or reinforce a climate of social approval of capital. That which is necessary in history is not always that which history brings, but at least we can see the rationale for the changes that were to shape the next period of capitalism, the period that extends into the present.

## V

As before, let us begin with a few stylized facts. All periods of boom require the stimulus of untrammeled investment possibilities, usually marked out by some major technical advance. The postwar period is no exception: I use the present tense because the period is still, so to speak, under our feet. Its technology is differentiated from that of the past by the application of laboratory science to the production process—the jet plane, plastics, the nuclear furnace, and above everything else, the enormous range of devices and equipment covered by "electronics," all bespeak an advance in the command over nature even more striking than that of machinofacture over the simple mechanized division of labor. It is an advance based on the integration of science and capital.

Once again a new level of technical capability has

brought new possibilities and imperatives for the circuit of accumulation. Profits depend heavily on scientific breakthroughs that give rise to temporary monopoly rents. Science further affects the organization of the firm by changing the character of the labor force on which it depends. Less reliance is placed on a homogenized mass of semiskilled operatives working on a mechanized assembly line, and more on a tiered structure of labor in which a professional or technically trained upper echelon designs and maintains the delicate, incomprehensible apparatus of production, while a lower tier performs the light, repetitive, and essentially monitoring tasks required to run it. Thus "high" technology can be profitably combined with low labor skills—one does not have to understand equipment whose output the worker "tests" but cannot directly alter or control.

Finally, the scale of capital has again expanded. The possibility of dispatching technical or managerial personnel around the world virtually overnight; of maintaining continuous contact with flows of production taking place in distant plants; of sending or receiving funds as easily as one can send or receive voice communication, have all combined to give wings to capital. Centers of advanced production arise in localities that were no more than coolie labor entrepôts during the last long wave. The label "Made in Hong Kong," stamped on commodities that embody the most remarkable capabilities of scientific production, becomes a symbol of the ability of capital to move wherever low labor costs or strategic sites for distribution offer competitive advantages.

An associated aspect of the internationalization of capital has been the rise of global finance, as the same technological advances give rise to international lending and capital-moving capabilities on a previously unknown scale. Paralleling the Hong Kongs of industry are the Caribbean centers of finance, key points of operation for flows of finance that move from nation to nation as interest rates or business expectations warrant. For the first time the social formation of capitalism has succeeded in bringing into being a realm of capital seemingly beyond all political control.

Thus the multinational industrial or financial corporation becomes the representative firm in this period, IBM or Citibank playing the paradigmatic roles of the pin factory in Smith's time and of U.S. Steel in the age of machinofacture. By the end of the 1970s, according to the Brandt Commission, such world-straddling industrial capitals accounted for one-quarter to one-third of the world's industrial production; comparable figures do not exist for banking, but they would certainly show an even larger degree of international size and concentration.[23]

Like previous periods, the present is also decisively marked by a change in the social structure within which accumulation occurs. The essential aspect of this change, as we already know, has been the vast enlargement of the economic role of the state. The military necessities of World War II, followed by the political necessities of the postwar era, provided the rationale—indeed, the imperative—first to enlarge, then to entrench a new level of government activity. Flows of government spending that

---

23. Brandt Commission, *North-South: A Program for Survival* (Cambridge, Mass.: M.I.T. Press, 1980), p. 187; Richard Barnet and Ronald Mueller, *Global Reach* (New York: Simon & Schuster, 1974), pp. 28–29, 270–271.

had averaged only 10 percent of total output in the 1920s rose by the 1960s to approach 30 percent and by the 1980s to exceed 50 percent of the total domestic expenditure of various nations. Throughout the capitalist world, governments undertook the management of demand through fiscal and monetary measures intended not only to avoid the disasters of the 1873–1893 period and the terrible depression of the 1930s but to maintain a high enough level of household spending to assure general prosperity. Growth became a central political preoccupation and gross national product a household phrase for the first time in history.

Thus the postwar period has witnessed an unmistakable change in the social structure of accumulation, as well as a decisive change in technological capability. Both brought positive effects at first. The new technology, buttressed by the state support of consumption, ushered in the longest-lasting and most powerful of all the long waves of expansion. In two decades Germany and Japan were transformed from war victims into economic "miracles." In the United States the severity of the business cycle was reduced to half that of the period 1900 to 1927 and to a quarter of its amplitude between 1900 and 1948.[24] In addition, the deliberate attempt to modernize and unify European capital laid the basis for a vast boom of commodification led by the automobile, which provided the long-sought replication of the American basis for economic patriotism. In the two centuries since Adam

---

24. From Walter Salant, "The American Economy in Transition," *Journal of Economic Literature,* June 1982, p. 568.

Smith's death the volume of world industrial production increased by over 500 times. Two-thirds of this increase occurred in the years between 1948 and 1971.[25]

But the enlargement of the physical capacities of production also brought unintended and undesired effects. As before, these were most immediately apparent in the sphere of competition. In the first years of the postwar boom the expansion of American capital abroad almost wiped out the European computer industry, and this was soon repaid by a devastating counterinvasion of foreign capital into the once-impregnable American steel and automobile markets. The movement of capital to the Hong Kongs of the world built up manufacturing capacity in these advanced outposts to 20 to 30 percent of their total outputs, a level not far removed from that of the industrialized world. However, the manufacturing capability of the newly industrializing nations was not mainly directed at satisfying the demands of their own markets but at invading the markets of other countries, including those of their own economic fatherlands. In similar fashion the internationalization of finance opened the way to the growth of a huge volume of international lending that was exceedingly profitable in its early stages and nearly disastrous when the postwar boom came to an end.

Not least, the workings of postwar capitalism soon gave rise to an endemic inflationary propensity that steadily gathered force until it threatened to annul the validity of the boom itself. It is not difficult to explain how capitalism

---

25. From W. W. Rostow, *The World Economy* (Austin, Tex.: University of Texas Press, 1980), p. 662.

became inflation-prone. The gradual widening and deepening of the intervention of the government into the workings of the economy, both as regards households and many sectors of business, radically changed the climate of expectations within which the accumulation process took place. Labor and business entered their market relationships with the secure knowledge that the hardships and risks of the past would not again be "permitted" to disrupt the process of growth. The presence of a large flow of government expenditure, by vastly reducing the likelihood of a cumulative fall of income for households and firms, tilted the direction in which labile expectations were expressed, from falling prices that anticipated deflation to rising prices that sought to guard against inflation. Without the threat of an actual or imminent recession, in the first decades of the boom there was no curb on the racheting movement of wages and corporate prices—the first outracing productivity, the second relatively indifferent to the normal constraints of demand—because businessmen were convinced that whatever buying power was needed would be provided by the fiscal and monetary powers of the state.

From this perspective the inflationary bias revealed the manner in which the accumulation process worked in a setting stripped of its traditional economic insecurity. For a while, as we have seen, the new setting encouraged strong real economic growth. But as the inflationary momentum began to feed upon itself, rising in the main capitalist countries from about 2 percent a year in the early 1960s to 10 percent by the end of the 1970s, the self-feeding process became a source of anxiety about potential self-destruction, not a reassuring testimony of underlying strength.

Strictly speaking the malfunction of inflation must be viewed as a political ailment—an aspect of the class struggle over shares—rather than as a direct expression of the logic of accumulation. For there was always an infallible means of bringing the malfunction to a halt. This was to limit the volume of income payments within a nation to the value of its output at unchanging prices. Any policy that capped the total payments of wages, rents, and profits (and that exerted a corresponding restraint on credit) could be counted upon to keep the price level stable. The difficulty, however, was that such a solution required the acquiescence of all classes or important interest groups. A few nations, such as Austria and Japan, and to a lesser extent Sweden, Switzerland, and West Germany, were able to approximate the requisite political consensus. The majority of nations, with the leading example of the United States, were not. As a consequence, the authorities in the inflationary nations were forced to pursue the only course open to them. This was deliberately to initiate a recession through restrictive monetary measures. First undertaken in Europe, then pursued with a vengeance in the United States, these policies did indeed reduce the rate of inflation by half in the early 1980s. The cost to the Western capitalist nations was, however, thirty million unemployed.

Thus we can see that inflation did not arise, as did depression, from a breakdown in the M-C-M' circuit. It arose as the consequence of moving the insecurity that previously kept the system under disciplinary pressure.

The pressure gone, the system revealed its susceptibility to monetary disarry. In this way the measures introduced to mitigate the deflationary instability of an unsupported accumulation process succeeded in their purpose, only to create the conditions for another kind of instability called inflation.

## VI

It is for these reasons that I have called the mounting difficulties of the late 1970s and early 1980s a crisis of intervention. The term refers not merely to the operational problems injected into the system because of its mixed, welfare character but also to the restrictions placed on state intervention as a means of resolving these problems. The crisis of intervention calls attention to the critical situation of our current sociopolitical dilemma, one not unlike that which preceded the merger wave at the beginning of the twentieth century. Today as then, evidence of a deep structural challenge can be discerned within the system, but the challenge is more feared and misunderstood than accepted and welcomed, and has progressed only far enough to reveal the limitations of the older structure, not far enough to force a solution for its problems. This applies not only to the crude measures with which inflation has been met but to the uncertain response to threats more directly connected with the accumulation process, such as the dislocations arising from the internationalization of capital, or to the menacing prospect of technological unemployment from robotization, or to the exercise of effective social control over the ecological side effects of production itself.[26]

In our coming chapter I will turn again to the response of modern capitalism to its current blockages and endangerments. But it is already clear that the logic of accumulation has returned us to the central concern of the worldly philosophers, for the capacity of capitalism to adapt to its self-generated strains and stresses is certainly a necessary condition for its historic continuance. Our survey of adaptational changes in the past has not yielded a line of sight into the future, but it has powerfully suggested that periodic institutional reorganizations are an integral part of the accumulation process, both emerging from its accumulated difficulties and pointing toward a new configuration capable of superseding these difficulties. This parallels the conclusions in Marx's work, where the central theme of his laws of motion—the outlook for capitalism itself—is left indeterminate, while subsidiary themes, such as the concentration of capital, assume sharp and precise importance. Thus the logic of accumulation can be expected to present its demands, although no one can say whether or not they will be adequately met.

Not surprisingly, then, our inquiry into what capitalism "is" turns in the direction of speculations about what capitalism may become or what may become of it. Having reached this point, however, I do not intend to make projections of the kind that the greatest economists have

---

26. What I am calling a crisis of intervention has been explored from various angles by a number of writers, among them James O'Connor, *The Fiscal Crisis of the State* (New York: St. Martin's Press, 1973); Jurgen Habermas, *Legitimation Crisis* (Boston: Beacon Press, 1973); Robert Reich and Ira Magaziner, *Minding America's Business* (New York: Harcourt Brace Jovanovich, 1982).

not succeded in doing with any great cogency. I do not believe that we can predict the life span of capitalism. We can, however, take up one last question that may clarify, even if it does not resolve, that central issue. This last question asks to what degree we can hope to understand the nature and logic of any social order and of capitalism in particular—how completely we can expect to explain the workings of social formations and with what confidence we can undertake the prediction of the social future in general. For the answers we can hope to gain from these Delphic inquiries surely depend on our right to pose such questions in the first place.

# 7

# The Limits of Social Analysis

IT IS HELPFUL to approach this daunting task by reminding ourselves that understanding, explanation, and prediction are universal attributes of human experience, not achievements of social science— never complete, but rarely completely inadequate. They are attained in varying degrees in differing social circumstances. Thus the problem for our consideration is not whether we can understand, explain, or predict at all the nature and logic of capitalism but the limits of our capacity to do so.

Let us begin with the matter of understanding, the bedrock on which all other functions stand. By understanding I refer to the fact that we create conceptual order out of the plenum of stimuli that impinge from without and arise within. Perhaps it is more accurate to describe understanding as the manner in which we impose order on this plenum, creating unities and patterns of perception in a universe that reason tells us is only a "buzzing, blooming confusion."

Our present interest does not lie in probing the mysterious capacity of understanding at its most elemental level of cognition but in stressing the critical role it plays in the analysis of society.[1] That critical role is to project meanings into webs of relationships among persons. We "understand" individuals in terms of their motives and intentions—as buyers, sellers, workers, capitalists; and we perceive behind their observed behaviors the presence of invisible structures such as property or markets. In turn, these structures can also be understood in different ways: a market can be seen as a locus of supply and demand, an instrument for advancing the circuit of capital, an arena of economic freedom, and in still other ways.

Thus to understand a society is to endow it with meaningful categories and relationships. Some of these come effortlessly and intuitively, because they have been taught to us in earliest childhood. Other elements of understanding arrive later, as the result of extended socialization processes through which we come to understand the "reality," and perhaps the "inevitability" or "rightness," of social attributes such as class differences. And some aspects of understanding are gained only at the expense of long study that finally leads us to "see" the presence of formerly unsuspected deep structures behind the façade of daily life.

The difficulty in reaching a general understanding of society is, of course, that the range of conceptual possibilities is much greater than when we seek to understand

---

1. See Alfred Schütz, "Concept and Theory Formation in the Social Sciences," in Maurice Natanson, ed., *Philosophy and the Social Sciences* (New York: Random House, 1963), p. 231f. and Peter Berger and Thomas Luckman, *The Social Construction of Reality.* (Garden City, N. Y.: Doubleday, 1966).

nature, although nature too can be perceived and under-stood in many ways.[2] These alternative possibilities arise from many sources, of which the most significant is proba-bly our position within the social formation: our private interest, influenced by material and moral considerations, is a powerful influence in forming our social perceptions. Beyond this unavoidable source of divergence, however, lie objective difficulties peculiar to capitalism. One of these is that the formation itself displays a wide range of tempo-ral variations (and intraperiod national differences), which requires that understandings must begin at a high level of abstraction, always a source of imprecision. In writing and in reading a study such as this one, one must constantly battle against the assumption that the configurations and institutions typical of capitalism in one's own country are depicted at a sufficient level of generalization to apply to those of all countries. This is an almost unavoidable source of error for assertions about the nature or logic of the system, many of which turn out to apply only to one nation, sometimes only to sections of that nation.

Second, we have stressed that in its essential nature, capitalism in all periods and national instantiations har-bors multiple ideologies rather than monolithic world views. Although these ideologies normally reinforce (or are at least compatible with) the acceptance of the regime of capital itself, the very existence of separated belief sys-tems robs the formation of that unchallenged unity of views it would otherwise enjoy. Unlike previous social formations, capitalism can be comprehensively viewed

---

2. See Paul Feyerabend, *Against Method* (London: Verso, 1975), Ch. 17.

from more than one perspective: as a social formation in which relations of production and distribution constitute the essential nature of the system; as a formation whose central organizing characteristic is the limitation of political power; as a society given its distinctive attributes by its prevailing rational-bourgeois mindset; as a civilization dominated by its technical apparatus; and in still other ways. Similarly, on a smaller scale the workings of the market mechanism can be perceived in what I have called the "decontaminated" form of individuals seeking to maximize their utilities, or as the manner in which the drive for prestige and power is sublimated in a milieu in which market relations have come to be imbued with significance far beyond the use-values that commodities confer.

Finally, there remains the elusive problem of the concept of capital itself, the central element of understanding around which this book is organized. It seems hardly necessary to state again the inherent complexity of the idea of capital. Marx's vast opus is an exhaustive exploration of the concept that is its title, and yet at its end, the idea of capital remains protean and elusive—not because of a failure of Marx's analytic powers but because those very powers have revealed the inherent dialectical aspects that render capital resistive to precise empirical formulations of a conventional kind.

It follows that the understanding of capitalism can never attain the clarity and precision of social formations in which there is only one angle of incidence of social vision, or where the central order-bestowing concept, such as kinship or kingship, is not intrinsically difficult to specify. This introduces an element of indeterminacy into our analysis at its very beginning point—an indeterminacy that will be incorporated in the explanations and predictions characteristic of the system. As we have been at some pains to insist, capitalism cannot be reduced to a determinist model—in part for reasons we already know but will explore further in the pages to come, at bottom because of the fundamental and inherent incompatibility of its nature with single-focused, sharply defined, and completely specifiable properties.

Such an inherently imprecise, subjectively vulnerable, and "unscientific" description of the manner in which we can understand capitalism collides head-on with the "positive" approach that prevails in contemporary mainstream economics. A positive approach means that we scrutinize society much as scientists examine nature, seeking to describe the social system in impersonal statements as if it were a part of physical reality. At its most ambitious, economics trys to depict capitalism as a system whose elements—"individuals" or "firms"—are treated as objects, and whose movements can be understood as the working-out of the generalized force of "maximizing utility" or "profit seeking." What is lacking in this description is any attempt to examine the manner in which these objects are themselves conceptualized in their social matrix. The individuals are presumed to create, or simply to harbor, the various desires and capabilities that form their utility goals; firms are mere shells that house largely unexamined activities of production in an unexplained pursuit of profit; the state has been reduced to a presence whose major function is to guarantee "private property" and "freedom of contract"; ideology has been banished; and a universal mentality of calculation, not belief, presumably gives the system coherence.

This is obviously a very incomplete, not to say unrealistic, specification of the nature of capitalism—that is, a highly restricted basis from which to understand the system. When this contrast between the real world and the model of that world is pointed out, the rejoinder of modern economics is that the purpose of social analysis lies in prediction, not in "understanding," and that prediction is interested only in whether premises yield confirmable results, not in whether they appear to be "realistic." Milton Friedman, the most influential exponent of this view, even holds that "in general, the more significant the theory, the more unrealistic the assumptions."[3]

The difficulty with this bold formulation is that it does not distinguish between the "unrealism" and the "abstractness" of assumptions on which theory is built. As Friedman recognizes, abstraction is necessary for all reasoned argument, and in general the power of argument increases with the degree that it sets aside the extraneous details of the "real world" to lay bare the causal or conceptual relationships beneath the surface. But this purifying procedure cannot be regarded as indifferent to the relation between the phenomena from which it begins and the abstractions at which it arrives. On the contrary, the search for abstraction seeks to discover the abiding behind the ephemeral, the essence within the appearance. This

---

3. Milton Friedman, "The Methodology of Positive Economics," in *Essays in Positive Economics* (Chicago: University of Chicago Press, 1953), p. 14.

effort cannot be described as "unrealistic," any more than manifestly unrealistic descriptions can be described as abstractions.

But what criteria can guide us in discovering abstractions or assumptions that will preserve the essential features of our social formation, when we have already stressed that capitalism is inherently susceptible to multiple interpretations? As we noted at the very outset, there is no method for guiding, or winnowing, the process of abstraction comparable to that which separates good hypotheses from bad ones on the basis of the predictions they yield. The conceptions that emerge from our understandings of society are always open to challenge and plagued by some degree of unclarity. They can neither be clearly "validated" nor falsified by history because we can never identify and allow for the effects of incidental or accidental elements that distort the workings of the assumptions whose consequences are presumably to be tested. There is no manner of identifying or calculating the resistance offered by society to the laws of motion of any element in it, as we can identify and measure the effect of air resistance to the descent of a feather.

All that can be said on behalf of the uncertain understandings on which we base, our analysis of capitalism, or of any other social formation, is that our understanding selects the problems to be examined, explained, and predicted, and that the test of the "realism" of those understandings is the clarification they generate. By clarification I mean a sense of historical placement, social and psychological penetration, and moral stability. This may seem a frail basis on which to rest our analytic efforts, but I believe it is the only one that is available to us, however wrong or blind one civilization's clarification may appear to another.

These considerations have an obvious bearing on the conception of capitalism as a social formation that we can understand, at least in part, by considering its nature and logic. It must by now be apparent that both "nature" and "logic" are heuristic and suggestive terms rather than empirically precise and definitive ones. Nevertheless I believe they enable us to understand the system—that is, to give it historical placement, social values, and psychological depth—in a manner that would not be attainable with more rigorously defined scientific or "positivist" approaches. The explanations and predictions that follow from these understandings will never have the clarity of those that follow from our conceptions of the natural world. But at least we will know that they represent, however imperfectly, a genuine confrontation with the problems of history, past and present, not mere intellectual conveniences or worse, playthings.

## II

Explanation is the effort to present a reasoned account of the interconnection of things.[4] There is one principal manner in which we accomplish this. It is to include that which is to be explained within a broader category of ideas

---

4. There are many ways of stating the problem of explanation. See Robert Nozick, *Philosophical Explanations* (Cambridge, Mass.: Harvard University Press, 1981), pp. 116–21; Carl Hempel, "The Covering Laws Analysis in Scientific Explanation," in I. Krimmerman, ed., The Nature and Scope of Social Science (New York: Meredith, 1969); Daniel Dennett, *Brainstorms* (Montgomery, Vt.: Radford Books, 1978), pp. 234–36; Norwood Hanson, *Patterns of Discovery* (New York: Cambridge University Press, 1975), pp. 54, 94–98.

or of events. If the category is one of ideas, the explanation is conceptual. We give reasoned accounts of concepts by describing them in general terms—for example, when we explain the social formation of capitalism by describing the various aspects of its nature.

The second kind of explanation is causal. Here the reasoned accounts follow mainly from assumptions with respect to the presumed regularity of certain sequences of occurrence—causes and effects. Thus we explain the logic of capitalism in terms of the manner in which actions of a given kind give rise to consequences of a given kind. These causal chains may be very simple, as when we postulate that the collective attempt to buy more of a commodity will raise its price, or they may be long and complex, as in the stimulus-response patterns that lead from the process of capital accumulation to the advent of some kind of crisis in the circuit of capital.

Conceptual explanation is obviously dependent on the understandings with which we grasp the totality of capitalism. I have spent enough time rehearsing the difficulties that attend this underlying process so that I need only add a word as to the way in which our understandings affect the specific conceptual explanations we proffer with respect to capitalism. To take a familiar example, the explanation of why we do or do not recognize capitalism as a social formation distinct from that of feudal society hinges directly on how we choose to understand the nature of each system. In the contemporary world the same criterion determines the explanations we adduce as to why modern-day "socialisms," in their northern or eastern European forms, are or are not variants of capitalism.

Everything hinges here on how we conceptualize such terms as capital, or how we perceive the nature of hierarchy, the autonomy of belief systems, and the like. As I have just been at pains to argue, there are no hard and fast rules with respect to these elemental concepts, so that disagreements can rage over matters that are, in the last analysis, beyond irrefutable demonstration.

It is causal explanation that requires to be more deeply examined. Causal explanation in the natural sciences usually rests on two assumptions. The first, as we have already noted, is that the event to be explained, such as the rate of descent of an apple or a feather, can be isolated or insulated from the effects of its surroundings. There is no way of determining the effect of a presumed cause, such as gravitation, on the rate of descent of objects unless we can wrench the event from its immersion in nature by conducting experiments in which, to complete the example, air has been completely removed from a tube so that feathers fall like stones. At best, such experiments are never perfect and the causal nexus retains some trace of uncertainty from contamination, and at worst the attempt to isolate and test the causal sequence is impossible or inapplicable.

Society is such a worst case. There is no way of observing social cause and effect in a pure environment, so a residue of indeterminacy obscures all causal generalizations—not because the causal nexus itself remains uncertain (that is the case, too, with natural events) but because the problem of identifying the elements to be included in that nexus is inherently indeterminate. That is one reason why presumed causal linkages in society, such as that between the dynamics of capitalism and war, do not explain—much less predict—events: Too much has been left out of the initial situation, or too much has been put in.

It is evident that our understandings directly affect this aspect of our explanatory difficulties. The elements of the historical situation that are left out or put in, and the way we describe these elements, depend on how we understand the situation to be explained. The relation of capitalism to war, for example, depends on whether we perceive capital as essentially an instrument for increasing productivity or for organizing labor power within the circuit of accumulation; on whether we see the state as an apparatus independent of, superior to, or in the thrall of the regime of capital; on our view of the mindset of the bourgeoisie and of the officials of the state: and so on. These are conceptual questions that establish the a problem to be explained as well as the cogency of the explanations that will be offered, since none can be "tested" as we test the explanations offered about the natural world. The reason that history remains always opaque to some degree—or perhaps more accurately, the reason that it remains a crystal with many facets—is precisely that it is capable of being understood from many vantage points, each of which raises for explanation its own questions, and each explanation of which is attended by the difficulty of specifying the elements that belong in its causal nexus.

This inherent indeterminacy of explanation is not unique to capitalism. There are different ways of explaining the fall of the Roman Empire, depending on the manner in which we understand that empire. What invests causal explanation with special interest for capitalism is that its specific behavioral attributes give to the system a resemblance to natural processes.

The laws of nature of the real world are those invariable characteristics or sequences that establish the orderliness of that world, ranging from the properties of subatomic particles and forces through molecular chemical valence and physical structure to large-scale regularities of celestial mechanics, or of random processes in general. To a degree that we often fail to appreciate, there are analogues of such regularities in society. These too begin at the "subatomic" level in presumably universal properties of cognition and other propensities, and build into "molecular" equivalents such as pair bonding and familial relationships, and into still larger structures of stable social organizations. The repeated demonstration of statistical patterns within human societies, applying to such diverse aspects as the size distributions of cities and organizations, the stubborn viscosity of income distributions, the "pendulum swings" of political sentiment, and the like, strongly suggest the presence of lawlike regulatory elements within human behavior, however unclearly these have been described.[5]

These lawlike aspects of behavior impart dependability to social formations—for example, the "routine" that is an indispensable order-bestowing aspect of all social systems. As Alfred Schütz and others have pointed out, these routines are the source of the predictable orderliness on which

---

5. See Albert Hirschman, *Shifting Involvements* (Princeton, N.J.: Princeton University Press, 1983) and Jan Pen, *Income Distribution* (New York: Praeger, 1971), p. 254f.

we depend when we drop a letter in the mailbox. They rest on the exercise of trust and belief, reciprocity and duty, without which the social process itself would not exist, and for which there is no analogue in the natural world.[6]

Capitalism adds only one new element to this source of order, but a new element of extreme importance. This is the generalized imperative of "rational" wealth seeking to which we have earlier paid heed. It is on the basis of this acquisitive drive that economics is able to build its remarkable explanations of social movements; the complex "scenarios" that can be constructed for capitalism exist only because it harbors and reflects this unique and powerful force. Regardless of the failure of modern-day economics to explain social evolution in the large, it is able to advance highly persuasive and partially testable explanations of social movements in the small, such as the dynamics of market prices, the response of production to these prices, the multiplicative possibilities of bank credit, the dependency of consumers' expenditures on the level of national income, the etiology and course of various kinds of crises; and a great deal more.

Indeed, the existence of this powerful behavior-orienting force leads to the possibility of viewing the social regulating properties as dominated by the "maximizing" impulse. At one end of the spectrum of these understandings is the reductionism of vulgar Marxism, where all social evolution is seen as proceeding in a mechanical

6. Alfred Schutz, "Common Sense and Scientific Interpretation of Human Action" in *Philosophy of the Social Sciences,* ed. M. Natanson (New York: Random House, 1963), pp. 324–25. See also Giddens, *Historical Materialism,* p. 154 and, from a different perspective, Fred Hirsch, *The Social Limits to Growth* (Cambridge: Harvard University Press, 1976), Ch. 10.

fashion from the self-expansion of capital; at the other end of the spectrum is the vulgar reductionism of modern theoretical economics, which perceives capitalism merely as a neutral field of property rights in which monadic individuals pursue their private utility-maximizing ends in the social vacuum that we have earlier described. It is often forgotten that the explanations that follow from this neoclassical mode of understanding embody a determinism as rigorous and ironclad as that of the most simplistic Marxism; and that economics itself becomes reduced to the "study of the formal implications of . . . relationships of means and ends on various assumptions concerning the nature of the ultimate data."[7]

Thus the indeterminacy that hampers causal explanations of capitalism because of the complexity and ambiguity of its nature is offset to some degree by the determinacy that guides its logic. In fact, however, the determinacy is considerably less than that of reductionist Marxist or neoclassical thinking. The behavior of the units of social analysis, taken as individuals, organizations, or social groups, departs in two important ways from the behavior of the units of the natural world. The first is that knowledge and intention are integral parts of the social universe, so that all behavior carries a volitional element, however submerged this may normally be. We discover this when social routines fail because the mail carriers go on strike, or when capitalists decide to take—or not to take—risks,

---

7. Lionel Robbins, *An Essay on the Nature and Significance of Economic Science* (London: Macmillan, 1932, 1972), p. 38. Classical economics also has its deterministic aspects, but these are leavened by the classical placement of the economic process within a class framework, inherently infusing the scenario with some degree of historic implication.

or to form political allegiances with liberal or conservative wings of government.

No less important is the indeterminacy that weakens the laws of behavior because of changes in social pressures that bear on, or direct, the maximizing impulse. Adolph Lowe has pointed out that the degree of determinism of behavior was probably far greater under early capitalism with its imperative need for work, its singleminded dedication to accumulation, and its small-scale units of capital than in modern capitalism, with its "discretionary" levels of income, imprecise strategic objectives for big companies, and huge commitments of unmovable investment. It is entirely possible that we live, as Lowe suggests, in a period when maximizing is losing its coercive force from below and its unequivocal guidance from above.[8]

What degree of causal explanation is then possible within capitalism? The preceding chapter illustrates the kinds of reasoned accounts we can give for some of its historical movements. Our analysis suggests that it is possible to explain many subprocesses and some important large-scale movements of the social formation, provided that we remain within the general framework of a given social structure of accumulation; but that crucial processes that alter the framework of accumulation may escape our anticipations and perhaps even our retrospective analysis.

Thus the explanatory schemas of the great economists are typically mixtures of success and failure. Smith and Marx both provide remarkable explanations of certain

---

8. Adolph Lowe, *On Economic Knowledge* (New York: Harper & Row, 1965; White Plains, N.Y.: M. E. Sharpe, 1977), Ch. 3.

sequences within the historical movement of the system—
for example, how the process of accumulation threatens to
block itself by bidding up the wages of labor; and both
further offer explanations of the manner in which the
spontaneous "maximizing" responses of the participants
avert this outcome. It is interesting to note that their
explanations differ, depending on their understandings of
the system. Smith's low estimation of working-class intelligence and his lack of interest in technological change
lead him to rely on a restoration of profits through blind
population effects. Marx, with his faith in the working
class and his emphasis on technological change as part of
the inherent tendency of capital, averts the crisis not by
the self-defeating population reflex of the working class
but through the actions of employers who introduce labor-
saving techniques, thereby cutting their own labor costs
and creating by their collective actions the manmade
equivalent of a population increase.

Each account throws an explanatory light over ways in
which the system "worked" during the period in which
they wrote, but the illuminations must be set against larger
failures, in particular Smith's lack of awareness of the
potential for industrial development or class strife, and
Marx's incapacity to foresee its potential use of state intervention. These too stem from conceptual limitation of
understanding, with respect both to the ideological and
political nature of the system and to its specific technical
and organizational adaptability.

Smith, for example, failed to see that in a regime of
capital the life energies of its guiding participants are of
necessity devoted to the discovery of ways of expanding
capital, so that a thousand economic generals are con-

stantly planning maneuvers to occupy high technological ground—not to mention the ten thousand soldiers with field marshals' batons in their knapsacks, the Arkwrights and Watts and Whitneys of all capitalist nations. Marx surely intended some such recognition when he wrote that "no social order ever perishes before all the productive forces for which there is room in it have developed,"[9] but even he did not sufficiently appreciate that the capacity for invention goes far beyond technical means to enfold the most seemingly incompatible institutions—national planning, nationalized enterprise, even the vocabulary and some of the techniques of socialism—into the service of the generation of capital. The laws of motion of capitalism as a social formation are not solely determined by the law of the tendency of the falling rate of profit or the law of the rising organic composition of capital or the expansive but self-regulating thrust of a society of perfect liberty. Rather, they reflect the interaction of these self-generated logics with other logics, above all those of political or ideological processes, that alter the ballistical properties of the social formation itself.

Against this sobering recognition of the limitations of causal explanation we must however pose a critical question: to what extent can we explain *noncapitalist* social formations? Anthropologists tell us there is much to understand, and therefore many reasoned accounts to offer, with respect to the nature of primitive societies. But what is there to explain with respect to their sleepwalking logic?

---

9. Marx, "A Contribution to the Critique of Political Economy," in Robert C. Tucker, *The Marx-Engels Reader* (New York: W. W. Norton, 1978), p. 5.

Or what of tributary societies? There is again a vast field for understanding with regard to the nature of imperial rulership in its many forms, but the trajectories of these formations can only be explained insofar as we can extend the motives of rulership into logics of power, not of impersonal, systemic movement. At one extreme the explanations of tributary systems are thus coterminous with those of biography; at the other, they are limited by our ability to understand class behaviors of "irrational" kinds, such as the fear and greed that drove the Roman upper classes to squeeze the middle and lower classes to the point of social collapse.[10]

Only within the social formation of capitalism can we still discover order-bestowing regularities that make it possible to analyze tendencies of the system without regard either to the inertias of primitive life or the biographical or "irrational" motives of tributary society; and to the extent that the state wrenches itself free of the regime of capital, or that modern affluent behavior obeys noneconomic motives, capitalism itself begins to lose its remarkable capacity for self-direction. As long as the circuit of accumulation remains the armature of the system, however, its tortuous sequences of M-C, C-C′, and C′-M′ will lend themselves to explanations that contain lawlike, calculable interactions that resemble those of the natural world.

It is therefore wrong to depict the limited reach of explanation as a failure of our analytic capabilities. It

---

10. See G.E.M. Ste. Croix, *The Class Struggle in the Ancient Greek World* (London: Oxford University Press, 1983).

is rather an accurate reflection of the bounded domain within which explicable behaviors are at work, as well as of the residual inexplicability that applies to behavior in general and to capitalist behavior in particular. The inadequacy of the reach of explanation is a measure of the degree to which capitalism still manifests the logics of older social formations or the growing presence of new ones; and the fact that explanation of a "scientific" kind is possible at all testifies once more to the inescapable necessity to regard capitalism as a social formation different from all others, not only by virtue of its nature but also by its logic.

What is remarkable, from this perspective, is not how little, but how much understanding can be conveyed with respect to capitalism by pursuing even its simple logic of accumulation. This logic, with its thrust and parry of productive forces and properties response, does not merely illumine the trajectory at some great distance but enters into its course with such immediacy that the development of the system would be robbed of all meaning without it. It would be difficult to write extensively about a logic of primitive societies or imperial kingdoms if the narrative were stripped of the particularities of this tribe or that kingdom, but it is of the essence of the grand logic of capitalism that it knows no national boundaries. The disruptive workings of a logic of accumulation, intertwined like the famous double helix with the unfolding of the struggle for political power and ideological clarity, apply to the developmental sequences of the United States as well as to those of England or Japan, a fact that surely testifies to the ability of the nature of capitalism to exert its persistent magnetic influence, not merely over the tapping of history's finger but over the pounding of its fist.

## III

Is it possible to predict the future of capitalism? Let us first distinguish between prediction and expectation. Prediction is the extension of explanation into the future. As such it relies on the presence of lawlike casual sequences whose operation is presumed to exert the same effects in times to come as in times past. Expectation is a much weaker kind of statement. It forms probabalistic conceptions of outcomes, drawing on generalizations and understandings, most of which do not embody formal causal propositions. It is the manner in which we make most of our plans with respect to the future, ranging from those made with near certainty on which we stake a great deal, even life itself, to those made tentatively, on which we act in guarded fashion. Our expectations end in uncertainty, the most psychologically difficult of all states, in which we can form no plans regarding the future and must act on the basis of blind faith, chance, or surrender to events.

It is clear that "scientific" predictions about the future of capitalism are impossible. The limitations of our causal explanations are too great. Prognosis with respect to the resolution of problems of the contemporary social structure of accumulation, and speculations with regard to possible configurations of the next structure, must be based to a very large degree on an amorphous amalgam of personal experience, political, social, and economic generalization, respect for contingency, and faith in human intelligence and will. For all the sophistication of eco-

nomic theory and measurement and of social and historical inquiry in general, the intellectual and emotional basis
on which we appraise the future is little more than such
a loosely knit tissue of frail wisdom, imperfect knowledge,
and variable hope.

Are there, despite these severe limitations, general expectations that can be held with respect to the future of
capitalism? I think there are, and that they are indicated
by the general implications of our investigation into the
nature and logic of capitalism. Here the first consideration
is the centrality of capital itself as the material and moral
basis on which the social formation is erected. To speak
about the future of capitalism is to speak about the future
of capital. This means the continuation, through whatever
technical and organizational means can be adapted for the
purpose, of the process of M-C-M', the perpetual-motion
machine that is the driving force of the system as well as
its historic badge of identity.

To gauge the likelihood that the circuit of capital can
continue requires that we make estimates of "impondera-
bles" of varying degrees of unknowability. Perhaps the
least difficult of these concerns the availability of new
avenues for investment to be opened up by the progress of
science. There seems little doubt that we have entered an
era of unprecedented penetration into nature's workings,
and that the scientific basis for an expansion of capital will
not be lacking. It is less certain, of course, that we have
also entered a new era of *profitable* penetration into nature, for many of the discoveries of science may not lend
themselves to commodification for a long time, if in-

deed ever. Nevertheless, insofar as a continuation of the M-C-M' circuit depends on an expanding technological capability, there is every reason to expect that the outlook for accumulation should be propititious.

A near-corollary follows from this prospect. It is that an advance in the productive forces of society seems likely to generate both material and social consequences of increasing disruptive magnitude. I do not have to review the contrast between the physical and social impacts of the pin factory, the steel mill, and the nuclear plant. What is important is that this widening impact of technology appears to require a corresponding widening of the defensive capability of society. As we have seen, this defensive capability is more and more exercised through the countervailing force of government, essentially the only means of protecting society from the undesirable side effects of accumulation, while also protecting the regime of capital from the consequences of the social damage that the accumulation process brings in its wake.

In all likelihood, then—although of course not with the assurance with which we can predict the outcome of a chemical reaction—the trend of capitalist society lies in the increased marshaling and deployment of the powers of the state, initially in support of the existing general structure of accumulation, later possibly as the vehicle by which the first tentative efforts may be made to go beyond that regime into another.

What other? That changes our focus from the relatively "logical" consequences of accumulation to the much less clearly defined question of the leap from one structure to another. Here there is no solid ground on which to rest expectations, comparable to the near-certainty with which we can anticipate a continued advance in the productive forces with their trains of social consequences. The movement beyond the confines of a given social configuration does not extend the logic of the preceding period but rather transcends it by moving into a new set of institutional boundaries and capabilities.

This does not always happen. The Dutch, poised at the very lip of becoming the first industrial capitalism, turned back from that risky course to enjoy the profits of trade and the leisured ways of an aristocratic culture, leaving the way open for England to seize the unoccupied terrain. At the middle of the nineteenth century, the English in turn lost their industrial hegemony when they were unable to abandon the restrained forms of British competition for the aggressive methods of corporate capitalism appearing in America.

In similar fashion, the United States today may turn away from, or find it cannot match, the organizational strategies of European and Japanese capitalisms that make increasing use of the state as a direct source of corporate capital and a means of penetrating foreign markets. So too the United States may continue to go against the tide that has steadily widened and deepened the social underpinnings of most advanced European capitalisms.[11] Thus despite the general drift toward an interpenetration of econ-

---

11. See Joseph Monsen and Keith Walters, *Nationalized Companies* (New York: McGraw-Hill, 1983) and Robert Kuttner, *The Economic Illusion* (Boston: Houghton Mifflin, 1984).

omy and state and a "socialization" of consumption, we cannot rule out the possibility that the United States will persevere in its efforts to disengage government from the economy and to shrink back its supportive functions. It is impossible to foresee what effects such a policy might have on the pace and strength of accumulation, but even if growth flourishes, the structural logic powerfully suggests that accumulation will continue to bring economic and social tensions and an encounter with the limits of the social framework—not because the process of amassing capital has faltered, but because it has succeeded.

Over the longer run, then, it still seems probable that the more successful capitalisms of tomorrow will be those that address the difficulties of the present period—its helplessness against the internationalization of capital, its propensity to inflation, its extreme social and ecological vulnerability to technological disruption—by new structures that utilize the state in various ways to cope with these problems as best they can be managed within a regime of capital. This raises the possibility that the most politically advanced capitalisms could become staging areas in which some of the institutions of capital, such as the market mechanism and autonomous enterprises, might be adapted to social control as part of a new, more "constitutional" regime of democratic socialism.[12] It is, alas, also the unhappy possibility that the very effort to create such a radical change would mobilize a resistance that would plunge the laboratory nations into chaos. As Perry Ander-

---

12. Alex Nove, *The Economics of Feasible Socialism* (London: Allen & Unwin, 1983).

son has observed, "No class in history immediately comprehends the logic of its own historical situation, in epochs of transition: a long period of disorientation and confusion may be necessary for it to learn the necessary rules of sovereignty."[13] These words, written about the advent of the Absolutist States of the seventeenth century, apply with equal cogency to the transitional period in which we live.

Thus the overall logic of the system—its historic destination—remains indeterminate because it hinges so largely on those opaque processes we mentioned at the beginning of our previous chapter—the confused struggle between the classes, the ebb and flow of technological advance, the adventures and misadventures of war. We have said what little can be ventured with regard to the outlook for investment. Nothing at all can be said as to the likelihood or the consequences of nuclear or ecological miscalculation other than that we are all hostages of a combination of premature technological virtuosity and persisting sociopolitical primitivism.

Perhaps the most elusive of these imponderable elements concerns the estimation of the regime of capital itself in the minds of the population at large. There has been a dramatic long-term trend toward social democratic governments.[14] At the same time there has been a widespread substitution of the state for capital as the target for

---

13. Perry Anderson, *Lineages of the Absolutist State* (London: New Left Books, 1974), p. 55.

14. Goran Therborn, "The Prospects of Labour and The Transformation of Advanced Capitalism," *New Left Review,* May/June 1984.

social resentment. Having legislated a mixed economy and a welfare system, the state is regarded as having "created" both, rather than as superintending at their births. As a result, the state becomes saddled with failures that arise not merely from inept administration and political bad judgment but from the unavoidable limitations that constrain the exercise of government within a regime of capital. The very real burdens of bureaucracy tend as a result to overshadow the problems of accumulation to which bureaucracy directs its attention, so that more animus is aroused by the failures of government remedies than by the malfunctions against which the remedies are directed, and more unrest is stirred by measures of taxation or environmental or other controls than by the shortcomings of the system from which arise the need for measures of redress. In this regard it is surely significant that the tenor of the political and ideological opposition in so many advanced capitalist nations is "antiestablishment" rather than"anticapitalist." In this way critical sentiments that might concentrate on the regime of capital are focused elsewhere, and the unchallenged domination of capital is fortified to a considerable degree—the United States as a case in point.

There is, in other words, no solid basis on which to rest expectations concerning the strength and stability of the central pillar of the social formation—namely, continued public acquiescence in the principle of capital itself. This critical area of blindness, robbing us of all sense of historical orientation where it is most needed, is itself in some measure the consequence of the political and ideological character of modern capitalism. The stabilizing influence of high culture has been largely drowned under the directionless flux of mass culture; impatience with the state has bred disrespect for government; cynicism is the only permanent residue from the floodtides of advertising. Thus the class struggle veers toward enlightenment at one moment and nihilism the next. Finally, and perhaps most important of all, there is the awareness brought home by the wild irrationalities of our time, many of them committed in the name of "Marxism-Leninism," that politics does not only move Left and Right, but also Up and Down, Forward and Back. And so we form our expectations as to the future, as I have just said, on the loosely-knit ties of frail wisdom, imperfect knowledge, and variable hope.*

These considerations are not intended to conclude our study in a miasma of uncertainty but rather to give a cutting edge to the expectations that are part of everyone's existence, at whatever level of abstraction or precise consideration. The cutting edge is supplied by the admonition that speculations about the future must begin with the nature and logic of the system as the observer understands them. I do not mean by this to insist on the cogency of my own conceptions of capitalism's nature and logic, but I am prepared to stake everything on an insistence that all

---

*My friend, the distinguished anthropologist Rudolpho Stavenhagen, talking about the blood spilled between Hindu and Moslem, Moslem and Jew, Protestant and Catholic, white and black, tribe and tribe; and the passions aroused by womens' rights and by eschatological views, once ruefully remarked to me, "And we thought this was going to be the century of clarification!"

future-oriented statements must begin with some such effort.

With respect to socialism in particular—that faded but still powerful lodestar—estimates about the future are worthless unless they consider the underlying substratum of human nature from which socialism, like all social formations, will have to draw its energy; unless they describe the main institutional means by which these energies will be shaped and channeled; unless heed is paid to the manner in which surplus is to be extracted and allocated, to the relation between economic and political functions, and to the content of belief systems. This is a task whose full achievement may lie beyond our grasp. But unless the task is attempted, the future of socialism can be only visionary or wishful, and the attempt to create a society that embodies its aspirations is likely to founder, as so often in the past, from a failure to appreciate the difference between making history and changing it.

Here I shall draw the line. The temptation is immense to present my own expectations as to the resilience and adaptability of capitalism as a social formation and of alternative historical formations that are imaginable or probable. But I shall resist. To show my own hand not only would instantly change the whole focus of this book but by revealing, as no doubt it would, the frailty of my judgments, would cast a shadow over the purpose to which these pages have been devoted. That purpose is the necessity to think through what capitalism is, prior to thinking about what it might become or what might become of it. I am prepared for the failures of analysis that these pages must inevitably contain, but my wager is that the mode of analysis itself is not a mistake. On that wager I must conclude these thoughts, at the very brink of the subject to which they naturally lead, and for which I hope they will be of use to others who follow them.

# Bibliography

THIS SHORT BIBLIOGRAPHY mentions most, but not all, of the sources cited in the text and a number not cited. It is not meant to be an exhaustive review of the immense literature that bears on this subject but to suggest a general range of reference. A few works of special importance for this book have been indicated with a dot (·).

---

- Amin, Samir. *Class and Nation.* New York: Monthly Review Press, 1980.

  Anderson, Perry. *Lineages of the Absolutist State.* London: New Left Books, 1974.

  ——— *Passages from Antiquity into Feudalism.* London: New Left Books, 1974.

- ——— *In The Tracks of Historical Materialism.* Chicago: University of Chicago Press, 1984.

  Appleby, Joyce Oldham. *Economic Thought and Ideology in 17th Century England.* Princeton, N.J.: Princeton University Press, 1978.

  Arrighi, G., Frank, A., & Wallerstein, Immanuel. *Dynamics of the Global Crisis.* New York: Monthly Review Press, 1982.

  Barnet, Richard & Mueller, Ronald. *Global Reach.* New York: Simon & Schuster, 1974.

  Bell, Daniel. *The Cultural Contradictions of Capitalism.* New York: Basic Books, 1976.

  ——— *The Coming of Post Industrial Society.* New York: Basic Books, 1973.

  Berger, Peter & Luckman, Thomas. *The Social Construction of Reality.* Garden City, N.Y.: Doubleday, 1966.

  Bergeson, Albert, ed. *Studies of the Modern World-System.* New York: Academic Press, 1980.

- Berman, Marshall. *All That Is Solid Melts into Air.* New York: Simon & Schuster, 1982.

# Bibliography

The Brandt Commission, *North-South: A Program for Survival.* Cambridge, Mass.: M.I.T. Press, 1980.

Braudel, Fernand. *Capitalism and Civilization.* New York: Harper & Row, 1981, 1982, 1984.

——— *The Mediterranean.* New York: Harper & Row, 1972, 1973.

Braverman, Harry. *Labor and Monopoly Capital.* New York: Monthly Review Press, 1974.

Chandler, Alfred. *The Railroads.* New York: Harcourt, Brace & World, 1965.

——— *The Visible Hand.* Cambridge, Mass.: Harvard University Press, 1977.

Cohen, G. A. *Karl Marx's Theory of History: A Defense.* Princeton, N.J.: Princeton University Press, 1978.

Coulanges, Fustel de. *The Ancient City.* Garden City, N.Y.: Doubleday/Anchor, n.d.

Deane, Phyllis. *The First Industrial Revolution.* Cambridge: Cambridge University Press, 1965.

Deane, Phyllis & Cole, W. *British Economic Growth.* Cambridge: Cambridge University Press, 1969.

Diamond, Stanley. *In Search of the Primitive.* New Brunswick, N.J.: Transactions Books, 1974.

Eichner, Alfred. *Why Economics Is Not Yet a Science.* Armonk, N.Y.: M.E. Sharpe, 1983.

Ewan, Stuart and Elizabeth. *Channels of Desire.* New York: Mc-Graw Hill, 1982.

Feyerabend, Paul. *Against Method.* London: Verso, 1975.

——— *Science in a Free Society.* London: Verso, 1978.

Faulkner, Harold. *The Decline of Laissez Faire.* New York: Holt, Rinehart & Winston, 1962.

Frank, A. G. *Crisis: In the Third World.* New York: Holmes & Meiers, 1980.

——— *Crisis: In the World Economy.* New York: Holmes & Meiers, 1981.

• Fenichel, Otto. "The Drive to Amass Wealth," *Psychoanalytic Quarterly,* January 1938.

Freud, Sigmund. Civilization and Its Discontents (1930). In Strachey, J., tr. and ed., *The Complete Psychological Works,* vol. XXI. New York: W. W. Norton, 1976.

——— The Future of an Illusion (1927). In Strachey, J., tr. and ed., *The Complete Psychological Works,* vol. XXI. New York: W. W. Norton, 1976.

——— Group Psychology and the Analysis of the Ego (1921). In Strachey, J., tr. and ed., *The Complete Psychological Works,* vol. XIX. New York: W. W. Norton, 1976.

• Fried, Morton. *The Evolution of Political Society.* New York: Random House, 1967.

Friedman, Milton. *Capitalism and Freedom.* Chicago: University of Chicago Press, 1962.

—— "The Methodology of Positive Economics," in *Essays in Positive Economics.* Chicago: University of Chicago Press, 1953.

Galbraith, John Kenneth. *The Affluent Society.* Boston: Houghton Mifflin, 1958.

—— *The New Industrial State.* Boston: Houghton Mifflin, 1967.

• Giddens, Anthony. *A Contemporary Critique of Historical Materialism.* Berkeley, Calif.: University of California Press, 1981.

Gordon, David. "Up and Down the Long Roller Coaster," in *U.S. Capitalism in Crisis.* New York: Union for Radical Political Economics, 1978.

• Gordon, David, Edwards, Richard, & Reich, Michael. *Segmented Work, Divided Workers.* New York: Cambridge University Press, 1982.

Habermas, Jurgen. *Legitimation Crisis.* Boston: Beacon Press, 1973.

Hanson, Norwood. *Patterns of Discovery.* New York: Cambridge University Press, 1958.

Hayek, Friedrich. *The Constitution of Liberty.* Chicago: University of Chicago Press, 1960.

Heilbroner, Robert. *The Limits of American Capitalism.* New York: Harper & Row, 1966.

—— *Marxism: For and Against.* New York: W. W. Norton, 1980.

—— *The Worldly Philosophers.* New York: Simon & Schuster, 1980.

Hempel, Carl, "The Covering Law Explanation in Scientific Explanation," in Immanuel Krimmerman, ed., *The Nature and Scope of Social Science.* New York: Meredith, 1969.

• Hirsch, Fred. *Social Limits to Growth.* Cambridge, Mass.: Harvard University Press, 1976.

• Hirschman, Albert. *The Passions and Interests.* Princeton, N.J.: Princeton University Press, 1977.

—— *Shifting Involvements.* Princeton, N.J.: Princeton University Press, 1980.

Hobbes, Thomas. *Leviathan.* Oxford: Clarendon Press, 1967.

Horvat, Branko. *The Political Economy of Socialism.* Armonk, N.Y.: M. E. Sharpe, 1982.

Hobsbawm, Eric. *Industry and Empire.* New York: Pantheon, 1968.

Huntington, Gertrude Enders. "Children of the Hutterites," *Natural History,* February 1981.

Kahler, Erich. *The Tower and the Abyss.* New York: Braziller, 1957.

Keynes, John Maynard. *The General Theory of Employment, Interest & Money* New York: Harcourt, Brace & Co. 1936.

Kuttner, Robert. *The Economic Illusion.* Boston: Houghton Mifflin, 1984.

Kondratieff, Nikolai. *The Long Wave Cycle.* New York: Richardson & Snyder, 1984.

• Lowe, Adolph. *On Economic Knowledge*. White Plains, N.Y.: M. E. Sharpe, 1977.

Locke, John. *The Second Treatise of Government*. Indianapolis: Bobbs Merrill, 1952.

Landes, David. *The Unbound Prometheus*. Cambridge: Cambridge University Press, 1969.

Lasswell, Harold. "The Triple-Appeal Principle: A Contribution of Psychoanalysis to Political and Social Science," *American Journal of Sociology*, January 1932.

Macpherson, C. B. *The Theory of Possessive Individualism*. New York: Oxford University Press, 1962.

MacIntyre, Alisdair. *After Virtue*. Notre Dame, Ind.: Notre Dame University Press, 1981.

Marx, Karl. *Capital*. New York: Vintage, 1977, 1981.

———— *Grundrisse*. Middlesex: Penguin, 1973.

———— *Economic and Philosophical Manuscripts of 1844*. New York: International Publishers, 1964.

———— *Pre-Capitalist Economic Formations*. New York: International Publishers, 1964.

• Mandel, Ernest. *Late Capitalism*. London: New Left Books, 1975.

———— *Long Waves of Capitalist Development*. New York: Cambridge University Press, 1980.

Mantoux, Paul, *The Industrial Revolution in the 18th Century*. London: Jonathan Capr, 1952.

Miliband, Ralph. *The State in Capitalist Society*. New York: Basic Books, 1969.

Mill, John Stuart. *Principles of Political Economy*. Toronto: University of Toronto Press, 1965.

Monsen, Joseph & Walters, Keith. *Nationalized Companies*. New York: McGraw Hill, 1983.

Nove, Alex. *The Economics of Feasible Socialism*. London: Allen & Unwin, 1983.

Noble, David. *America by Design*. New York: Knopf, 1977.

Nozick, Robert. *Philosophical Explanations*. Cambridge, Mass.: Harvard University Press, 1981.

O'Connor, James. *Fiscal Crisis*. New York: St. Martin's Press, 1973.

Ollman, Bertell. *Alienation: Marx's Conception of Man in Capitalist Society*. Cambridge: Cambridge University Press, 1971.

Piore, Michael & Sabel, Charles. *The Second Industrial Divide*. New York: Basic Books, 1984.

Pen, Jan. *Income Distribution*. New York: Praeger, 1971.

Reich, Robert and Magaziner, Ira. *Minding America's Business*. New York: Harcourt Brace Jovanovich, 1982.

Rieff, Phillip. *Freud: The Mind of the Moralist*. New York: Viking, 1959.

Robbins, Lionel. *An Essay on the Nature and Significance of Economic Science.* London: Macmillan, 1972.

Reynolds, Lloyd. "The Spread of Growth to the Third World," *Journal of Economic Literature,* June, 1982.

Rostow, W. W. *The World Economy.* Austin, Tex.: University of Texas Press, 1980.

• Sahlins, Marshall. *Stone Age Economics.* Hawthorne, N.Y.: Aldine, 1972.

——— *The Use and Misure of Biology.* Ann Arbor, Mich.: University of Michigan Press, 1976.

Ste. Croix, G.E.M. *The Class Struggle in the Ancient Greek World.* Ithaca, N.Y.: Cornell University Press, 1981.

Salant, Walter. "The American Economy in Transition," *Journal of Economic Literature,* June 1982.

• Shaikh, Anwar. "Economic Crises," in Tom Bottomore, ed., *A Dictionary of Marxist Thought.* Cambridge, Mass.: Harvard University Press, 1983.

——— *Crisis Theories in Economic Thought.* London: Thames Polytechnic, 1977.

• Schütz, Alfred. "Common Sense and Scientific Interpretation of Human Action" and "Concept and Theory Formation in the Social Science", in Maurice Natanson, *Philosophy and the Social Sciences.* New York: Random House, 1963.

Schumpeter, Joseph. *Capitalism, Socialism, and Democracy.* New York: Harper & Row, 1946.

——— *Business Cycles.* New York: Mc-Graw Hill, 1939.

——— *The Theory of Economic Development.* Cambridge, Mass.: Harvard University Press, 1949.

Schelling, Thomas. *Micromotives and Macrobehavior.* New York: W. W. Norton, 1978.

Schudson, Michael. *Advertising: The Uneasy Persuasion.* New York: Basic Books, 1984.

Schonfield, Andrew. *Modern Capitalism.* New York: Oxford University Press, 1965.

——— *The Use of Public Power.* Ed. Zuzanna Schonfield. New York: Oxford University Press, 1982.

Smith, Adam. *The Wealth of Nations.* Oxford: Clarendon Press, 1976.

——— *Lectures on Jurisprudence.* Oxford: Clarendon Press, 1978.

——— *Theory of Moral Sentiments.* Oxford: Clarendon Press, 1976.

Sombart, Werner. *Why Is There No Socialism in the United States?* (White Plains, N.Y.: International Arts and Sciences Press, 1977.

Tawney, R. H. *The Acquisitive Society.* New York: Harcourt, Brace & Co., 1948.

Taylor, George. *The Transportation Revolution.* New York: Holt, Rinehart & Winston, 1964.

*213*

# Bibliography

Therborn, Goran. *What Does the Ruling Class Do When It Rules?* London: Verso, 1980.

—— "The Prospects of Labour and the Transformation of Advanced Capitalism," *New Left Review,* May/June 1984.

Thompson, E. P. *The Making of the English Working Class.* New York: Random House, 1974.

—— *The Poverty of Theory.* New York: Monthly Review Press, 1978.

• Wallerstein, Immanuel. *Historical Capitalism.* London: Verso, 1983.

—— *The Modern World-System.* New York: Academic Press, 1974, 1980.

Weber, Max. *Economy and Society.* New York: Oxford University Press, 1947.

—— *General Economic History.* Glencoe, Ill.: Free Press, 1950.

White, Lynn. *Machina Ex Deo: Essays in the Dynamics of Western Civilization.* Cambridge, Mass.: M.I.T. Press, 1968.

Wood, Ellen Meiksins. "The Separation of the Economic and the Political in Capitalism," *New Left Review,* May/June 1981.

—— "Marxism and the Course of History," *New Left Review,* September/October 1984.

Wright, Erik Olin. *Class, Crisis and the State.* London: Verso, 1979.

Weeks, John. *Capital and Exploitation.* Princeton, N.J.: Princeton University Press, 1981.

# Index

accumulation of capital, 33, 42–78,
  141–43, 197–99, 203
  and abstractness of money capital,
    55–56
  class dominance and, 65–67
  commodification aspect of, 60
  division of labor in, 154–55
  "economic patriotism" and, 167,
    169
  fixed capital, 145–47
  individual achievement and, 115
  inputs for, 101–3
  logic of, *see* capitalism, logic of
    imperatives of, 142–43
  mechanization and, 155
  necessity of, 52–58
  power and, 51–52
  preconditions for, 142–43
  and production of use-values, 62
  profits and, 71–72
  self-preservation and, 58
  social restraints on, 62–63, 147
  social structure of, 149–53
  state support of, 89–90
  structural changes in capitalism
    from, 145–47
acquisitive behavior:
  aggressive aspect of, 59
  Christianity and, 109, 112–13
  consequences of, 110, 113–14
  in ideology of capitalism, 108–17
  as *le doux commerce,* 110
  moral significance of, 113–16
  nature of capital and, 59
  protection of capital and, 59–60
  science of, 110–11, 192
*Acquisitive Society, The* (Tawney),
  62n

advertising, 118, 137
*Advertising: The Uneasy Persuasion*
  (Schudson), 118n, 137n
*Affluent Society, The* (Galbraith),
  62n
*After Virtue* (MacIntyre), 115n
*Against Method* (Feyerabend), 182n
Amin, Samir, 28n, 82, 107
*Ancient City, The* (Coulanges), 133n
Anderson, Perry, 29n, 204
Appleby, Joyce Oldham, 107n
Aristotle, 34
  on limitlessness of wealth, 56
Arkwright waterframe, 155

behavior, human:
  determinacy of, 193–94
  maximizing, 63–64
  self-preservation in, 58
  volitional element in, 193–94
  *see also* acquisitive behavior;
    domination
Bell, Daniel, 80–82
Bentham, Jeremy, 114–15
Beres, David, 21n
Berger, Peter, 181n
Bergeson, Albert, 95n
Berman, Marshall, 136
*Bradstreet,* 163
*Brainstorms* (Dennett), 187n
Brandt Commission, 172
Braudel, Fernand, 15, 20, 35–36
Braverman, Harry, 162n
Briggs, Asa, 159
business life, 16–18

capital, 33–52
  abstract, 55, 183

*215*

capital *(continued)*
  as central organizing principle of
    capitalism, 79, 83–85. *See also*
    regime of
  concentration of, 92, 163–64
  continuous transformation of,
    36–38
  defensive tactics of, 151, 163
  defined, 36–37
  dependency and, 41–42
  dissolution and recapture of, 56
  international movement of, 94–95,
    171–72
  as material things, 36
  money, 36–37, 55–57, 92, 163–64
  organization of, 150
  political freedom and, 127–28
  power of, 39–40, 46, 51–53, 76
  regime of, 52–77, 82, 204–5
  size of, 150, 160, 164, 171
  as social process, 36–42, 57
  tradition and command vs., 37–
    38
  vulnerability of, 56–58
  *see also* accumulation of capital;
    fixed capital; ideology of
    capital; M-C-M' formula for
    capital; protection, of capital
*Capital* (Marx), 13, 42$n$, 147$n$
capitalism, *see also* capitalist
    development
  capital as central organizing
    principle of, 79, 83–85
  causal explanation in, 194–97
  competition and, *see* competition
  configurations of, 61, 182
  contradictions of, 80–83
  definition of, 13–16
  determinacy of, 189–90, 192–94
  and domination, 39–42, 47–48, 141
  energy of, 136–37
  expansion of, 36, 61, 127, 197
  as explained by economics, 184–85
  fetishism in, 17, 111–12
  and ideology, *see* ideology of
    capital
  logic of, 19, 31–32, 52, 58, 142–43,
    145–47, 188, 198–99
  masking of functions in, 97–98,
    105–6
  mercantile, 14–15, 87–88
  multiple perspectives on, 182–83
  nature of, 16–19, 31–32
  power and, *see* power

  predictions for future of, 142–45,
    199–207
  and privatization of politics, 100
  profit in, 76–77, 142–43
  rationality in, 55
  as regime of capital, 52–77, 82,
    204–5
  self-ordering tendency of, 61–64,
    105
capitalist development, 148–79
  chart of, 150–52
  class struggle and, 149
  crises in, 149–53, 162–63, 166–67
  in Europe vs. U.S., 167–70
  intervention and, 177–78
  long waves in, 148–49
  productive expansion vs. social
    restriction in, 148
capitalist development, first period
    (1760–1848) (nascent industrial
    capitalism), 154–60
  competition as disciplinary force
    in, 156–57
  division of labor in, 154–55
  labor deployment in, 161
  precapitalist sector in, 156
  productivity in, 154–56
  social aspect of, 155–56, 158–59
capitalist development, second
    period (1848–1893), 160–70
  capital concentration in, 164
  cartels, trusts, and mergers in, 163
  changes of scale in, 164
  crisis in, 162–63
  economic patriotism in, 167–68
  intensification of competition in,
    162–63
  labor deployment and
    homogenization in, 161–62
  market saturation in, 162
  organizational changes in
    production and, 160–62
  political confrontations in, 167–
    69
  response to crisis in, 163–64
capitalist development, third period
    (1893–1941), 164–70
  crisis in, 165–67
  economic patriotism in, 167–69
  labor and fixed capital in, 165
  political confrontations in, 167–69
  price competition and, 165–66
  response to crisis in, 166–67
  revitalization in, 166

capitalist development, fourth period
(1941–) (postwar period), 170–77
changes in social structure during,
172–73
crisis in, 177–78
expansion of scale of capital in,
171
global finance in, 171–72
inflation in, 174–77
international lending in, 174
and state, 204–5
technology in, 170–71
capitalists:
and dissolution and recapture of
capital, 56–57
market processes and, 62–63, 65
maximizing behavior of, 63–64
misers vs., 52
and self-preservation, 58
state power and, 127–28
as universal class, 132
Carnegie, Andrew, 162
cartels, 163
cash nexus, 64
Census of Manufactures (1869), 156
Chandler, Alfred, 163n
*Channels of Desire* (Ewen and
Ewen), 168n
"Children of the Hutterites"
(Huntington), 139n
Christianity, and acquisition of
wealth, 109, 112–13
*Civilization and Capitalism*
(Braudel), 15
*Civilization and its Discontents*
(Freud), 21n
Claessen, H., 50n
class:
bourgeoisie as, 131–32
ruling, 129–32
struggle, 149
universal, 130, 132
working, 167–70
*Class and Nation* (Amin), 28n
*Class Struggle in the Ancient World,
The* (Ste. Croix), 197n
coercion, 38–42, 47, 48, 141. *See also*
domination
Cohen, Ronald, 50n
Colbert, Jean Baptiste, 88
commerce, as civilizing, 110
commercialization, 117–18
commodification, 60, 118, 139–40
of ideas, 137–39

commodities:
fetishism of, 17, 111–12
ideas as, 137–39
commodity chains, 90–91, 93–95
*Communist Manifesto*, 64, 136
competition:
defined, 57
development of, 150
as disciplinary force, 58, 63–64,
156, 162–63
and dissolution and recapture of
capital, 57
human nature and, 57–58
residual profit and, 70
self-preservation and, 58
"Concept and Theory Formation in
the Social Sciences" (Schütz),
181n
concentration of capital, 92, 163–64
corporations:
fixed costs of, 162
supranational, 94, 172
Coulanges, Fustel de, 133n
Council of Vienne (1311), 109
"Covering Laws Analysis in
Scientific Explanation, The"
(Hempel), 187n
crisis of intervention, 177–78
*Cultural Contradictions of
Capitalism, The* (Bell), 80–82
cultural realm, 81–82, 84–85, 132–40
and commodification, 137, 139–40
ideas as commodities in, 137–39
natural world as seen in, 133–37

democracy, liberalism and, 125–29
democratic socialism, 15, 203–5
Dennett, Daniel, 187n
dependency, 41–42
infantile, 48–49
social relationships and, 41–42
Depression, Great, 169
*Dialogue of the Common Laws, A*
(Hobbes), 93n
Diamond, Stanley, 28n
*Discourse on Property, A* (Tully), 69n
discipline, 97–100, 103f, 128, *see also*
economic patriotism
distinction, *see* prestige
distribution, 85–86, *see also* wages,
profits
division of labor, 154–55
domination, 38–40, *see also* coercion
in animals vs. humans, 47

# Index

domination *(continued)*
  capital accumulation and, 42
  and capitalism, 39–42, 74–76, 99, 141
  infantile dependency and, 48–49
  by merchants, 39–40
  in primitive society, 38–40
  state vs. economic, 90–92
  as structured inequality, 47–48
  in tributary systems, 86–87
  universal class and, 130
  of women, by men, 49n
Duby, Georges, 108n

Early State, The (Claessen and Skalnik), 50n
East India Companies, 88
economic calculation, 97
"Economic Crises" (Shaikh), 146n
*Economic Illusion, The* (Kuttner), 202n
economic patriotism, 167, 169
economic realm:
  activities of, 96
  boundaries of, 124–25
  emergence of, 87–89
  function of, 96–97
  government and, 122–25
  and ideology of capitalism, 116–17
  labor allocation in, 98–100
  political aspect of, 97–100, 103f
  political realm and, 85–90
  power in, 90–95, 98–100
  rights in, 129
  state's maintenance of, 101–3
  in tributary systems, 85–87
economics, 110–12
  capitalism as explained by, 184–85
  development of, 109–12, 151
  and fetishism of commodities, 111–12
  on origin of profits, 111–12
  positivist approach in, 184
  rational wealth seeking and, 192
  reductionism of, 193
  social analysis and, 185
  as social engineering, 97
  surplus ignored in, 111
*Economic Thought and Ideology in Seventeenth-Century England* (Appleby), 107n
Edwards, Richard, 161, 162n
Engels, Frederick, 64, 95, 136–37, 158, 168

equality, de jure, 89
equilibrium, general economic, 17
Europe:
  economic patriotism, 167–69
  inflation in, 176
  logic of capitalist development in, 168–70
*Evolution of Political Society, The* (Fried), 43n, 50n
Ewen, Stuart and Elizabeth, 168n
expansion of capitalism, 36, 61, 127, 197
explanation, 187–91
  causal, 188–91
  conceptual, 188–89
  indeterminacy and, 189–91
  limitations of, 197–98
  understanding and, 188–89
exploitation of labor, 74–76, 99

feudalism, 87–88
Feyerabend, Paul, 182n
finance, global, 171–72
*Fiscal Crisis of the State, The* (O'Connor), 178n
fixed capital, 146–47
  vs. variable, 35
Frederick II (the Great), King of Prussia, 88
freedom:
  capital and, 127–28
  economic, 66–67
  intellectual, 139
  political, 125–29, 131, 139
Freud, Sigmund, 21
Fried, Morton, 43n, 50n
Friedman, Milton, 125, 185
*Future of an Illusion, The* (Freud), 21n

Galbraith, John Kenneth, 62n
Gay, Peter, 21n
Giddens, Anthony, 93n, 127, 137n, 192n
Glorious Revolution (1688), 122
goods and services, 36
Gordon, David, 148–49, 161, 162n
government: *see also* state
  bourgeois view of, 119–22
  economic realm and, 122–25
  expansion in postwar period, 172–73
  individuals and, 119–22
  laissez faire and, 122–23

legitimacy of, 119–20
liberal view of, 120–23
popular views of modern, 204–5
property rights and, 101
regulatory intervention by, 166
social democratic, 204–5
government spending: increases in, 172–73
inflation and, 175
*Group Psychology and the Analysis of the Ego* (Freud), 21n

Habermas, Jurgen, 178n
Hanson, Norwood, 187n
Hegel, Georg Wilhelm Friedrich, 130
Hempel, Carl, 187n
Hirsch, Fred, 192n
Hirschman, Albert, 56n, 109–10, 191n
*Historical Materialism* (Giddens), 93n, 192n
Hobbes, Thomas, 93, 119–20
on competition, 57
homogenization of labor, 161–62
horsed nomads, 50–51
Horvat, Branko, 127n, 131
human nature:
competition and, 57–58
oppressive social relationships and, 29, 38–40, 47–49, 74–76, 99, 141
social systems shaped by, 20–22
Huntington, Gertrude Enders, 139n

ideas:
as commodities, 137–39
ideologies: *see also* cultural realm
defined, 107
developmental view of, 151–52
explanatory function of, 107
multiple, under capitalism, 182
as ruling class explanation, 107, 117
science as, 135
surplus and, 108
as "world" religions, 107–8
ideology of capital, 107–40
acquisitiveness in, 108–17
commercialization and, 117–18
individuals in, 120–22
natural world as seen in, 134–37
political freedom and, 125–29

and private vs. public sectors, 116–17
protective complexity of, 139–40
and relationship of government to economy, 122–25
and relationship of liberalism and democracy, 125–29
rulership in, 129–32
science in, 135–36, 140
*Income Distribution* (Pen), 191n
incomplete tributary societies, 87
individuals:
conformity and, 128
government and, 119–22
in ideology of capitalism, 120–22
unconscious and, 21–22
indoctrination, social, 23–24
industrial capitalism, *see* capitalist development
Industrial Revolution, 155
*Industrial Revolution in the 18th Century, The* (Mantoux), 42n
inequality:
profits and, 65–66
wage labor and, 66–67
infantile dependency, 48–49
inflation, 174–77
government spending and, 175
as political ailment, 176
innovation, technological, 73
inputs, for accumulation of capital, 101–3
insatiability, 51–52, 54
*In Search of the Primitive* (Diamond), 28n

James, William, 44
Japan, 92, 173

Kahler, Erich, 137n
Keynes, John Maynard, 142, 144
Kuttner, Robert, 202n

labor:
allocation of, 98–100
deployment of, 161–62
developmental view of, 150
discipline and command of, 98–100, 128
division of, 154–55
in early capitalism, 158–61
exploitation of, 74–76, 99
fixed capital and, 146–47, 165
high technology and, 171

# Index

labor *(continued)*
  homogenization of, 161–62
  industrial employment for, 157–58
  liberal view of, 151
  as process vs. commodity, 72
  and reification of natural world,
    134–35
  relationship of capital to, 66–74
  surplus value of, 72–73
  wage, 66–73, 82
*Labor and Monopoly Capital*
  (Braverman), 162*n*
laissez faire, 122–23
Landes, David, 161
Lasswell, Harold, 21*n*
*Late Capitalism* (Mandel), 75*n*
*Lectures on Jurisprudence* (Smith),
  101*n*, 114
legitimacy, political, 81–82
*Legitimation Crisis* (Habermas),
  178*n*
lending, international, 174
Lenin, V. I., 162
*Leviathan* (Hobbes), 57, 93*n*, 119–20
liberalism, 120–23
  democracy and, 125–29
  labor as seen by, 151
  laissez faire and, 122–23
*Lineages of the Absolutist State*
  (Anderson), 29*n*
livelihood, access to, 44–46
Locke, John, 68–69, 101
  on purpose of government, 122
  on unlimited acquisition, 112–13
logic: *see also* capitalism, logic of
  of economic vs. political power,
    90–95
  of primitive societies, 28
  of social systems, 18–19, 24–32
  of tributary societies, 29
  long waves, 148–49
Lowe, Adolph, 194
Luckman, Thomas, 181*n*

machines:
  hand-built, 155
  machine-made, 160
MacIntyre, Alisdair, 115*n*
Macpherson, C. B., 69*n*
Magaziner, Ira, 178*n*
*Making of the English Working
  Class, The* (Thompson), 159*n*
management, specialization of, 160
Manchester weavers, 158

Mandel, Ernest, 75*n*, 148–49
Mantoux, Paul, 42*n*
market, system, 16
  emergence of, 87
  human contact reduced in, 59
  labor exploitation in, 99
  in liberalism, 121
  multiple perspectives on, 183
  regulatory functions of, 62–63, 65,
    69
  requirements of, 61–63
Marx, Karl, 34, 136–37, 142, 165,
    167, 178, 183
  on evolution of capitalism, 143–
    44
  historical sequences explained by,
    194–95
  on labor as process vs.
    commodity, 72
  limitations in theories of, 195–96
  on power of money, 44
  on primitive accumulation, 42*n*
  on profits, 71–73, 144
  on wage slavery, 58
Marxism:
  capital accumulation in, 147
  cash nexus in, 64
  dependency in, 41
  domination in, 40
  fixed capital in, 146–47
  M-C-M′ formula in, *see* M-C-M′
    formula for capital
  political freedom in, 126
  reductionism of, 192–93
  social formations in, 18
  surplus value of labor in, 72–73
  technological rents in, 73–74
"Marxism and the Course of
  History" (Wood), 147*n*
*Marxism: For and Against*
  (Heilbroner), 139*n*
mass production, 161
maximizing behavior, 63–64
M-C-M′ formula for capital, 36, 127,
    197
  breakdowns in, 165
  commodities enhanced in, 59–60
  competition and, 57
  development of, 150
  disciplinary force generated by,
    61–63
  fixed capital, 146–47
  identification of, 160
  profits and, 65, 72–73, 200–1

Index

scientific breakthroughs and, 200–201
state power and, 93–94
vulnerability of capital in, 56–58
mechanization, 155
*Mediterranean, The* (Braudel), 20, 35
mercantile capitalism, 14–15, 87–88
merchants:
  domination by, 39–40
  emergence of, 87–88
  power of, 40–41
  profits of, 65–66
mergers, 163–64
*Micromotives and Macrobehavior* (Schelling), 115n–16n
military power, 92
  economic activity encouraged and protected by, 103
  property rights "legitimized" by, 50
Mill, John Stuart, 142
  on exploitation of labor, 75
  on laissez faire, 123
  on profits, 71
  on "stationary state" of capitalism, 143
*Minding America's Business* (Reich and Magaziner), 178n
misers, 52
money:
  as abstract, 55
  as basis of measurement of prestige, 55
  as intermediary in trade, 37
  power of, 44
money capital, 36–37, 55–57, 92, 163–64
Monsen, Joseph, 202n
morality, state power restrained by, 84–85
multi-axial principle, 80–83
*Multinational Companies and Nation States* (Murray), 104n

*Nationalized Companies* (Monsen and Walters), 202n
nature, 191, 193
  in Judeo-Christian tradition, 133–34
  reification of, 134–35
Nozick, Robert, 187n

O'Connor, James, 178n
"One World or Three?" (Worsley), 94n

Paris Commune, 168
*Passions and the Interests, The* (Hirschman), 56n, 190–10
patriotism, economic, 167, 169
*Patterns of Discovery* (Hanson), 187n
peasants, 42, 68
Pen, Jan, 191n
*Philosophical Explanations* (Nozick), 187n
political economy, 110–11
*Political Economy of Socialism* (Horvat), 127n
political power, 90–95
  in economic realm, 98–100
  logic of, 90–93
  production and, 100
political realm, 81–82, 84–90
  boundaries of, 124–25
  and constitutional constraints on state, 89
  economic functions in, 101–6, 151
  economic realm and, 85–90
  and ideology of capitalism, 116–17
  labor discipline and, 99–100
  labor exploitation and, 98–99
  rights in, 129
  in tributary systems, 85–87
*Political Theory of Possessive Individualism, The* (Macpherson), 69n
*Politics* (Aristotle), 56n
population growth and wages, 70–71
postindustrial society, 15
*Poverty of Theory, The* (Thompson), 80n
power, 45–52
  of capital, 39–40, 46, 51–53, 76
  capital accumulation and, 51–52
  defined, 46
  expansion of, 50–52
  insatiability and, 51–52, 54
  of institutions, 39–40
  legitimation of, 49–50
  military, 50, 92, 103
  of money, 44
  political vs. economic, 90–95
  prestige vs., 44–45
  in private vs. public spheres, 100
  psychic roots of, 46–49

221

power *(continued)*
  self-preservation and, 58
  of taxation, 89–90
  wealth and, 45–46
  *see also* domination; political
    power; state power
predictions, 185, 199
  expectations vs., 199
  for future of capitalism, 142–45,
    199–207
  for socialism, 207
prestige:
  desire for, 43
  money as basis for measurement
    of, 55
  power vs., 44–45
  self-preservation and, 58
  wealth and, 42–46, 53
prestige goods, 43–45
  in U.S., 168
  wealth vs., 44–45
  workers and, 64, 168
price agreements, 163
price competition, 165–66
price leadership, 165–66
"primitive accumulation," 42*n*
primitive societies, 27–28
  kinship in, 79
  prestige in, 44–45
private property, 59, 101
  ownership of, 38
  as potentially protective, 127, 128
  state and, 50, 59, 101, 122
  technological rents and, 74
production, 36, 85–86
  organizational changes in, 160–62
  political power and, 100
  surplus in, 33–34, 66
  of use-values, 62
  wage labor and, 67–69
productivity:
  fixed capital and, 146–47
  growth of, in industrial period,
    154–56
  social and material disruption
    from increases in, 201
profits, 65–77
  accumulation process and, 71–72
  capital-labor relationship and,
    66–74
  commodity chains and, 91
  decline in rate of, 144
  as driving force of capitalism, 142
  economics and, 111–12

exploitation and, 75
inequality and, 65–66
and logic of capitalism, 76–77, 142
M-C-M' formula and, 65, 72–73
as merchants' gains, 65–66
political benefits from, 98
population growth and, 70
as residuals, 70, 74
Schumpeterian, 73–74
as successful exercise of political
  relationship, 76–77
as surplus value, 72–73
technological rents and, 73–74
technology and, 171
from trade, 65–66
as value added, 69–73
wage labor and, 67–73
proletarianization, 42*n*, 157–58, 161
property, *see* private property
protection, of capital, 58–60
protectionism, 163
*Protestant Ethic, The* (Weber), 56*n*
public works, 101–3

railroads, fixed costs of, 162
reductionism:
  dangers of, 79–80
  of economics, 193
  of Marxism, 192–93
regime of capital, 52–77, 82, 204–5
Reich, Michael, 161, 162*n*
Reich, Robert, 178*n*
religion, science vs., 135
representation and participation,
  81–82
Ricardo, David, 69–71
right of refusal, 66–67
Roman empire, collapse of, 87
ruling class, 129–32, *see also*
  domination
Russian Revolution, 131–32, 168
Rustow, Alexander, 50–51

Sahlins, Marshall, 43*n*, 47*n*
Ste. Croix, G. E. M., 197*n*
scarcity, wealth and, 46
Schelling, Thomas, 115*n*–116*n*
Schudson, Michael, 118*n*, 137*n*
Schumpeter, Joseph, 14, 142
  on evolution of capitalism, 144
Schumpeterian profits, 73–74
Schütz, Alfred, 181*n*, 191–92
science, 135–36, 140
  as ideology, 135–36, 140

role of, in capital accumulation, 152, 200–1
*see also* technology
scientific management, 162
*Second Treatise on Government* (Locke), 68–69, 112–13
*Segmented Work, Divided Workers* (Gordon, Edwards and Reich), 162n
Shaikh, Anwar, 146n
*Shifting Involvements* (Hirschmann), 191n
Skalník, P., 50n
Skocpol, Theda, 94n
Smith, Adam, 13, 34, 101, 142, 154
  on acquisitiveness, 109–10
  on competition, 156
  on Deity, 17, 54
  on dependency of workers, 41, 65
  on government power, 122–23
  historical sequences explained by, 194–95
  on industrial employment, 57–58
  on inequality, 46
  on life span of capitalism, 143
  limitations in theories of, 195–96
  on moral costs of wealth accumulation, 113–14
  on profit, 69–71
  on pursuit of capital, 54
  on social approval of wealth, 42–43
social analysis, 78–84, 180–208
  abstraction in, 185–86
  causal explanation in, 188–91
  clarification as test for, 186–87
  conceptual explanation in, 188–89
  economics and, 185
  indeterminacy of, 183–84
  natural world and, 191, 193
  positive approach to, 184
  reductionism and, 79–80
  and regime of capital, 82
  understanding in, 180–84
  unrealism in, 185–86
  validation as impossible for, 186
*Social Construction of Reality, The* (Berger and Luckman), 181n
social formations, 13–32, 78–84
  central organizing principle of, 79, 83
  conflict between groups in, 30
  contradictions of, 82–83
  human unconscious and, 21–22

levels of complexity in, 25
logic of, 18–19, 24–32
nature of, 18–24, 30–32, 61
noncapitalist, explanation in, 196–97
orderliness of, 191–92
primitive, 27–28
socialization process in, 23–24
surplus and, 34
tradition and command vs. capital in, 37–38
tributary, 28–29, 197
usefulness of descriptions of, 31
social indoctrination, 23–24
socialism:
  democratic, 15, 127n, 131, 203–5
  intellectual freedom and, 139
  managerial, 144
  predictions for, 207
socialization process, 23–24
*Social Limits to Growth, The* (Hirsch), 192n
social position, 65–67
  and accumulation of capital, 65–67
  exploitation and, 74–76
  *see also* class; dependency
Sombart, Werner, 167
sports, commercialization of, 117–18
state:
  accumulation of capital supported by, 89–90
  activities of, 96
  constitutional constraints on, 89
  economic function of, 101–3
  economic power ceded by, 89–90
  emergence of, 49–51
  as influenced by capitalism, 84–85
  in modern capitalism, 170–77, 202–5
  political function of, 96
  private property and, 59, 101, 122
  and public works, 101–3
  role of, 78–106
  in scenarios of capitalism, 105
  unprofitable economic necessities provided by, 101–3
  war and, 50–51
  *see also* government
state power:
  capitalists and, 127–28
  domination and, 38–40
  economic power vs., 90–95
  evolution of, 49–51

# Index

state power *(continued)*
over international commodity
chains, 93–95
marshaling and deployment of,
201–3
M-C-M' formula and, 93–94
morality as restraint on, 84–85
Stavenhagen, Rudolpho, 206n
Stone, Lawrence, 15n
*Stone Age Economics* (Sahlins), 43n
*Studies of the Modern World-System*
(Bergeson, ed.), 95n
surplus, 33–34
allocation of, to capital-owning
class, 67–76
economic vs. political power and,
90–92
exploitation and, 74–76
in feudalism, 87
ideology and, 108
origins of, 75–76
in tributary societies vs.
capitalism, 34–35, 98
use of, to augment power, 35
*see also* profits
surplus value, 72–73, *see also* profits

Tawney, R. H., 62n, 64, 100
taxation, power of, 89–90
Taylor, Frederick, and Taylorism,
162
technological rents:
profits and, 73–74
property rights and, 74
technological unemployment, 146–
47
technology:
development of, 150, 160
labor and, 171
in postwar period, 170–71
production as force of, 22
profitability of, 200–201
technoeconomic structure, 80–82
social systems and, 22–23
temporary monopoly rents from,
171
*Theory of Moral Sentiments* (Smith),
109–10
Therborn, Goran, 107n
Thomas, Keith, 15n
Thompson, E. P., 79–80, 159n
*Thoughts on War* (Freud), 21n
*Three Orders, The* (Duby), 108n
Tocqueville, Alexis de, 64, 158

*Tower and the Abyss, The* (Kahler),
137n
trade, 36
money as intermediary in, 37
profits from, 65–66
tributary societies, 28–29, 197
centralized rulership in, 79
domination in, 86–87
economic domain in, 85–87
feudalism and, 87
hierarchies in, 79, 86–87
ideologies in, 107–8
incomplete, 87
legitimacy of government in, 119
logic of, 28–29
political realm of, 85–87
political vs. economic logic in,
91–92
self-preservation in, 58
surplus in, 34–35
"Triple Appeal Principle, The"
(Lasswell), 21n
trusts, 163–64
Tully, Jas., 69n

underdeveloped countries, 90–91, 94,
130, 170–71
understanding, 180–84
conceptual explanation and,
188–89
defined, 180
role of, in social analysis, 180–82
unemployment, technological,
146–47, 170–71
United States, 173
economic success in, 167–68
inflation in, 176
logic of capitalist development in,
167–168
mass consumption goods in, 168
predictions for capitalism in,
202–3
working class allegiance in,
167–68
universal class, 130, 132
*Use and Abuse of Biology, The*
(Sahlins), 47n
use-values, 34, 37, 62
utilitarian philosophy, 115

Veblen, Thorstein, 53, 64
vertical integration, 163
*Visible Hand, The* (Chandler),
163n

wage contracts, 66, 69
wage labor, 66–73, 74–76, 99
wages:
  and employment, 157–58
  population growth and, 70–71
  profit and, 69–73
wage slavery, 68
Wallerstein, Immanuel, 90–91, 94, 130
"Wallerstein's World Capitalist
    System" (Skocpol), 94*n*
Walters, Keith, 202*n*
war:
  capitalism and, 190
  organized states and, 50–51
Watt steam engine, 155
wealth, 33–37
  and access to livelihood, 45–46
  as capital, 34–35, 55, 64
  conditions necessary for existence
    of, 45–46
  extraction of, from productive
    society, 33–34
  individual's pursuit of, 17
  as limitless, 55–56
  market requirements and, 61–63
  power and, 45–46
  prestige goods vs., 44–45
  and prestige or distinction, 42–46,
    53

  scarcity and, 46
  social approval of, 42–43
  surplus as, 34
  use-values of, 34, 37, 64
*Wealth of Nations, The* (Smith), 13,
    34*n*, 101, 109–10, 114, 154
Weber, Max, 14, 55, 56*n*, 134
*What Does the Ruling Class Do
    When It Rules?* (Therborn),
    107*n*
White, Lynn, 134
*Winding Passage, The* (Bell), 80*n*
Wood, Ellen Meiksins, 100, 147*n*
workers:
  dependency of, 41–42
  enforced competitiveness and,
    63
  maximizing behavior of, 63–64
  prestige goods and, 64
  self-preservation and, 58
  wage labor and, 66–67
working class:
  in Europe, 168–70
  in U.S., 167–70
"world-economy," 94–95
World War II, 172
Worsley, Peter, 94*n*

Zukier, Henri, 21*n*